# THE COMPLI
# COOKBO(
# TEEN CHEFS

200 simple step-by-step recipes and essential techniques to inspire young cooks

Margaret A. Wheat

# TABLE OF CONTENTS

# INTRODUCTION

Hearty welcome to the world of taste..! Despite being a necessary life skill, cooking is a funny way to spend time with family and trying new healthy foods. Whether or not you're new to kitchen, this book is just for you. Cooking is definitely an art which can be mastered through consistent practice. The more you practice, the better the outcome will be. Basic plan in this book is dishes you can make all in all without any other person. The harder the plans the more help will require. The recipes and activities in this book are all kid attempted and kid-upheld.

The kitchen can be an exciting spot for even small children. They see adults working enthusiastically over there; watch the steam ascend from pots and aroma what's on the menu that dinner. It is not generally beneficial to welcome them into the kitchen to help, yet consider doing as such whenever time allows. Additionally,

Teens might see the wonderful chance to additionally foster their cooking capacities for when they'll need to cook for themselves. You might be enthusiastic about attempting different food varieties. If you are keen to go through this book, no doubt you have an excellent interest in cooking or planning to take your capacities to a more elevated level.

Once you practice these recipes, you will indeed transform into am expert home cook who can make an evolving collection of dishes. I believe that by exploring this book, you'll bloom into a gifted Teen Chef who has everyone in your gathering keen to see what you baked straight away! This book will assist you in mastering the fundamental skills to thrive in the Kitchen and will indeed guide you to become a Little PRO in cooking. Nevertheless, being safe is at most important to a happy cooking session, since follow the kitchen rules strictly for a Happy Cooking Folks..!

# CHAPTER 1: UNDERSTANDING KITCHEN BASICS

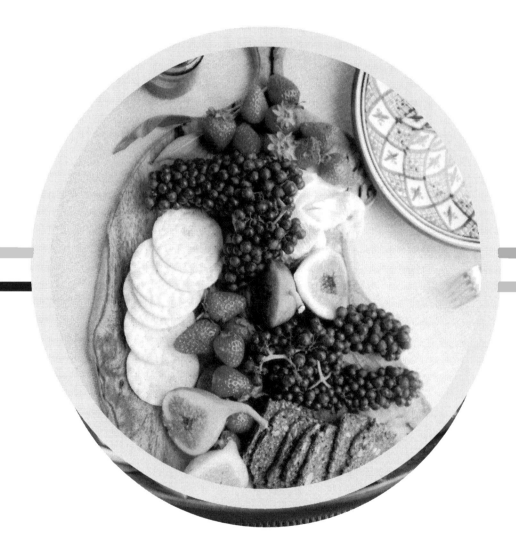

# Kitchen Guidelines for Adolescences

You have your hands washed, ingredients organized and your measuring spoons ready. But before you start, it's a good idea to learn a few kitchen rules. It's easy to get injured in the kitchen if you're not cautious, and a cut or burn will put an end to your exciting cooking session. Follow the Kitchen guidelines for a happy Kitchen session!

* **Always get an adult supervision.** These recipes are made for children to enjoy, but you always need a grown-up to help. Normally this is a stage utilizing the broiler, oven, food processor, heated water, or any assignment that could be unsafe to do all alone.

* **Wash your hands.** Clean hands are the most useful tool in the kitchen! It's essential. Wash your hands which will foster extraordinary kitchen cleanliness practice. You must always do so after touching any raw meat or poultry to prevent cross contamination. Before baking as well, always wash your hands with soap and warm water. But don't rush. Make sure your hands are truly clean by washing atleast 10 seconds.

* **Wear suitable clothing.** Roll up those sleeves; get your apron on and your oven mitts at the ready. Ensure you don't have hanging gems or free streaming sleeves, and keep long hair tied back. Wear suitable clothing. Roll up those sleeves; get your cover on and your broiler gloves primed and ready It's likewise a smart thought to pop shoes on, By chance that things get thumped or hot fluids get spilt.

* **Handle poultry and meat safely.** Continuously clean up your hands subsequent to raw meat and poultry handling. Refrigerated eggs can be left on the counter for as long as two hours prior to heating. Bringing them up to room temperature can assist with preparing. However, you don't have to do that for any other recipes.

* **Use potholders.** The broiler or oven is hot! It will burn your skin suddenly (same for any dish coming out), so consistently ask an adult for a hand. Try getting a towel or potholder for a secure holding of hot vessels.

* **Prepare your work area.** Prior to beginning any baking, set up every one of the fixings on a spotless, level work area. your measuring cups and spoons prepared, snatch a bowl, and ensure pan is handy. Thus you will save time and distraction of missing a key ingredient.

* **Practice the knives session primarily.** Initially, try practicing -cutting and slicing session- using plastic or less sharp knives. Then, you will gradually learn the proper way to use a knife.

* **Wipe the chaos straightway.** Keep a wet cloth and a trash bowl on the counter. Wipe up any spills as they occur and clean your space between ventures depending on the situation. You'll save time with regards to cleanup at the end.

* **At last, learn medical aid in emergency.** Learn when to use plasters and where store them, as well as how to treat minor burns by running cold running water from a tap over the burn for ten minutes. After this, you should remove any jewelry or clothing near the burn and wrap it in Clingfilm to keep clean.

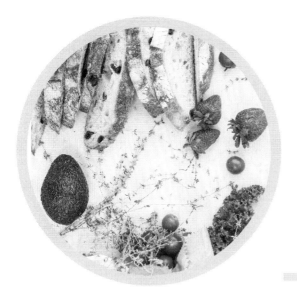

# Tips to Become a Good Cook

Go through the 10 tips and implement them while cooking next time. Make them say Wow..!

**1** Research and read the recipe. Read the recipe several times. Go through the steps of the recipe mentally before gathering your ingredients and tools to start cooking.

**2** Exercise the recipes frequently. Practice makes always perfect. When it comes to cooking as well, frequent practice makes you perfect in making dishes and you will get appreciated for your hard work in the kitchen.

**3** Stay structured. A well-prepped workspace, free of clutter, is a strong foundation for success in the kitchen. No one likes to deal with a messy kitchen after making a lovely meal. Wiping down counters, clearing your cutting board, and disposing of nonessential items as you go will make the kitchen clean without worrying about a huge mess at the end.

**4** Prep your ingredients first. Before turning the oven on, make sure that all your ingredients are prepped. Did you notice culinary experts start cooking, after ensuring everything is accessible. Measure and chop your ingredients before you begin cooking, and have them at your workstation, ready to go.

**5** Slow and steady to win Cooking. Slow and steady practice is relevant when it comes to cooking as well. Always take time to make recipes- prepping ingredients, adding each ingredient in time and allowing them to hit the correct temperature to make the recipe ready.

**6** Do not over task your food. This is as important as the previous tip. Overworking on your dough while baking will squeeze out the pockets of air that make foods light and fluffy. Instead, combine ingredients until sufficiently mixed, and allow your dough to come to room temperature before putting it in the oven.

**7** Taste every so often! Don't wait until a dish is almost finished, because flavor is built up in layers. Taste the food early on as you begin to cook a recipe, and taste throughout as you add ingredients. But, do not taste dishes containing raw or undercooked meats or eggs. Wait until they are fully cooked and then taste.

**8** Be persistent. A recipe formula doesn't generally work out completely the initial time, and that is alright. The next time you attempt it, you can apply what you figured out how to deal with it all the more skillfully. You'll likewise get the satisfaction of realizing you stayed with it!

**9** Use fresh ingredients. While new foods grown from the ground are a significant piece of a flavorful dish, so are fresh spices and toasted spices: They can transform a simple meal into one that sings with their bright, aromatic qualities.

**10** Watch others cooking. Observe and learn from people you admire in cooking skill. The more you apprehend, the broader your own skill set will become.

# Kitchen Safety Tips

It's cool to get caught in excitement of a holiday recipe however before you get in to the Kitchen, ensure it's safe with the following tips.

* Wash your hands with soap before cooking and after touching raw meat or eggs.

* When using oven, stove or sharp knives an elder person should be near. Since those can be dangerous. Always ask for help if you're in doubt.

* Don't leave the kitchen while the stove or oven is on.

* Always turn off the stovetop and oven when you're done cooking.

* Assume that anything on the stove or in the oven is hot. Use oven mitts.

* Tie your hair back. It can get into your food and block your view!

* Turn the handles of pots and pans away from you. An accidental push can send a pot flying and cause a dangerous spill.

* Never let ingredients you eat raw (such as berries) touch foods you will cook (such as eggs).

* Never eat raw batter or dough. Wait until food is cooked before tasting.

* Use a food thermometer to check whether food is cooked in apt temperature. Check safe minimum temp-chart.

* Unplug the machines like blenders and toasters right after you use them.

* Refrigerate leftover food promptly at 40°F or below

# Understanding Nutrition
# Values in Food

Food naturally contains nutrients— like protein, fat, and carbohydrates—that deliver energy. A few nutrients, like fiber and sodium, don't provide energy but are significant for wellbeing. Your body needs the right mix of nutrients to work appropriately and grow. We've given the per-serving amount of each of these nutrients in every recipe so you know what you're eating. Here are a few terms to get familiar with nutritional information:

CALORIES The total amount of energy in your food is termed as Calories. It comes from fat, protein, or carbohydrates. The amount of calories you need per day depends on your age, size, and activity level.

PROTEIN Essential macro nutrient build from essential amino acids, which come from food. Helps in body building and repairing muscles, blood, and organs. Meat, poultry, fish, eggs, beans, lentils, nuts, and seeds are protein rich.

FATIs an important nutrient that your body uses for Hormone function, memory and certain nutrient absorption. Vegetable and nut oils, which provide essential fatty acids and vitamin E. Healthy fat is found in avocados and seafood. Saturated fat comes from animal sources like red meat, poultry, and full-fat dairy products, should be limited.

CARBOHYDRATEIs your body's main source of energy, which highly found in fruits, vegetables, and milk, as well as in sugar. Body use it as a fuel and Each gram provides 4 calories.

SODIUM   It is a mineral found in many foods. It's needed for normal muscle and nerve functions.  It keeps the fluids balanced in the body. High sodium consumption leads to fluid retention, high blood pressure, heart disease and stroke.

Nutrients are weighed in grams (g) and milligrams (mg). One teaspoon of water weighs 5 grams; one teaspoon of sugar weighs about 4 grams.

# Let Us Learn Measuring Ingredients

Our recipes depend on the correct ratio of ingredients (the amount of one ingredient in relation to another)—plus chemistry—to work. But you don't have to be a scientist to bake like a pro. Just follow these simple rules:

## Dry Measuring

☒ Use the right Measures—metal or plastic measuring cups for dry ingredients, and glass or clear plastic measuring cups with spouts for liquids.

☒ Spoon dry ingredients (like flour, cornmeal, unsweetened cocoa, and sugar) into the dry measuring cup until it are overflowing. Before measuring flour, loosen it with a fork or spoon in the bag or container. Do not pack flour down or tap the measuring cup. Level off the excess flour with a straightedge (like the back of a knife or a metal spatula).

☒ Firmly pack brown sugar into a dry measuring cup and level it off. It should hold its shape when turned out of the cup. Flour should be kept in a wide-mouth jar or bag for ease.

Choose a measuring cup that fits the amount you need. With a scoop or spoon, fill the cup until it overflows. Do not pack the flour down or use the measuring cup to scoop the flour, as it will cause compression. Using the straight edge of a butter knife, level the flour even with the rim of the measuring cup.

## Liquid Measuring

Measure liquids in a spouted, transparent measuring cup set on an even surface. Pour liquid so that it reaches the measurement line. Be sure your eyes are even with the level of the measurement. If need be, bend down to read the measurement at eye level.

☒ Place your liquid measuring cup on the countertop. Make sure your eyes are at the same level as the measuring marks. Pour the liquid into the cup until its right at the mark—not above or below.

☒ Use measuring spoons, not eating utensils, to measure small amounts. For dry ingredients, scoop the measuring spoon into the container until the ingredient is overflowing, then level it off. For liquid ingredients, pour liquid until it reaches the top edge of the spoon.

# Equivalent Measurements

| | |
|---|---|
| Dash | less than ⅛ teaspoon |
| 1½ teaspoons | ½ tablespoon |
| 3 teaspoons | 1 tablespoon |
| 1 cup | ½ pint |
| 2 cups | 1 pint |
| 4 cups (2 pints) | 1 quart |
| ¼ pound | 4 ounces (113 g)s |
| ½ pound | 8 ounces |
| ¾ pound | 12 ounces |
| 1 pound | 16 ounces |
| 4 tablespoons | ¼ cup |
| 5 tablespoons plus 1 teaspoon | ⅓ cup |
| 8 tablespoons | ½ cup |
| 10 tablespoons plus 2 teaspoons | ⅔ cup |
| 16 tablespoons | 1 cup |

# Safe Temperature Chart

| Protein | Safe Internal Temperature |
|---|---|
| Beef, pork, veal and lamb (roast, steaks and chops) | 145°F with a three-minute "rest time" after removal from the heat source |
| Beef, medium-rare (warm red center) | 135°F* |
| Eggs and egg dishes | 160°F, but cook eggs until both the yolk and the white are firm; scrambled eggs should not be runny |
| Beef, medium-well (slightly pink center) | 150°F* |
| Beef, well-done (no pink) | 160°F* |
| Ground beef | 160°F |
| Pork, medium-rare | 145°F(63°C) plus a 3-minute rest |
| Pork, medium | 150°F |
| Pork, well-done | 160°F |
| Ground pork | 160°F |
| Fish | 140°F |
| Chicken | 165°F(74°C) |
| Turkey | 165°F(74°C) |

To ensure food safety, ground beef should be cooked to a minimum of 160°F. Check and ensure with a meat thermometer, as color alone is not a secure indicator

# How to preserve foods in Kitchen

Food preservation helps in preventing growth of microorganisms and slowing the oxidation of fat; which increase the shelf life. Let us learn to make food preserved by following the below methods.

## FOOD PRESERVATION METHODS

| | | |
|---|---|---|
| Drying | Tie them together and hang in a sunny spot away from any humidity as a preservation technique for removing moisture. Modern method of drying is to use an electric dehydrating machine. | Preserving herbs, fruits, vegetables and meats |
| Salting | Salt is added to products, mainly meat and fish, to draw out moisture. | Preserving beef jerky and dry salted cod |
| Canning | Sterilise your cans and glass jars in simmering water for a few minutes. Then fill with things like jam. After filling, place the lid on firmly. Lower the jars into a pot full of water cover and bring to a boil. Process for about 10 minutes. Pull the jars out of the hot water and let it cool. Vacuum seal as they cool. | Preserving fruits, vegetables and meats. |
| Pickling | Soak your vegetable, ex. most famously cucumbers, in a brine with salt transfer them to a jar full of vinegar and add salt. Vegetables undergo a fermentation process, which also results in a vitamin boost. Pickled vegetables are known for having an increased level of vitamin B6. | Preserving fruits, vegetables and meats. |
| Freezing | Electric freezers to preserve our foods. | Preserving most fruits and some vegetables, but meats and fish fair well |

# CHAPTER 2: COOKING METHODS AND KITCHEN TOOLS

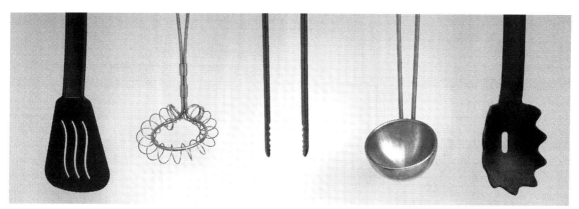

# A to Z Kitchen Tools

1    Blender- Having a Blender on hand helps in making smoothies and or salad dressings quickly.

2    Bowls-Mixing Bowls are inexpensive will last a lifetime.

3    Can Opener-Please ask an adult for help when using one to open a can. The lid from an open can has a very sharp edge.

4    Citrus reamer- A kitchen tool, often wooden, with a cone-shaped "blade" and deep troughs that extracts juice from citrus fruit.

5    Colander- A bowl with holes throughout used to drain pasta and canned foods and to rinse fruits and vegetables.

6    Cutting Board -Provides a flat, level surface for chopping, slicing, or dicing ingredients. Often made of plastic or wood, look for one big enough for you to comfortably use your knife.

7    Knife- Look for a chef's knife for cutting any fruits or veggies and a serrated knife (with a scalloped blade) for cutting breads and cakes.

8    Knife Sharpener-Once you have the right knife, you'll need to keep it sharp using Knife Sharpener

9    Ladle -A deep-bowled spoon with a long handle. It's ideal for transferring soup, gravy, or stews from a pot to serving bowls.

10    Ice pop molds- Containers that give shape to liquid ingredients as they freeze. Filling small paper cups or yogurt containers—or even ice cube trays—works in a pinch.

11    Ice-Cream Scoop -A useful tool to get similar portions of cookie batter.

12    Measuring Cups and Spoons -Plastic measuring cups and spoons will do just fine, but stainless steel ones are more durable. For wet measurements, look for a Pyrex glass measuring cup.

13    Metal Spatula- Helps remove baked goods from a sheet pan.

14    Mixing Bowls- A set of 4 stainless steel, glass, or plastic bowls in different sizes will do nicely for most recipes.

15    Measuring cups Kitchen tools made of plastic, metal, or glass used to measure liquid or dry goods like flour or sugar.

16    Measuring spoons-Small kitchen tools, often made of plastic or metal, used to measure small amounts of liquid or dry ingredients, such as spices, salt, and extracts.

17    Meat thermometer- A device inserted into meat to measure its internal temperature and gauge "doneness," helping you to not overcook. It's useful for cooking steaks and roasts to temperature and for safely cooking poultry and pork.

18    Melon baller- A utensil that produces sphere shapes from melons and other produce. It's also used to scoop seeds from

vegetables, make mini scoops of cookie dough or ice cream, and shape truffles.

19   Mortar and pestle -A tool consisting of a bowl and a club-shaped implement used to crush seeds, spices, herbs, and vegetables.

20   Offset Spatula -A metal spatula whose handle attaches with a crook slightly above the blade to make frosting a cake easier.

21   Oven-Safe Gloves -For taking things in and out of the oven safely.

22   Parchment Paper -Used to line the bottom of pans and helps keep your baked goods from sticking to them or making a mess.

23   Pastry Brush -For brushing liquids onto doughs, crusts, and finished baked goods.

24   Plastic Wrap- Useful for refrigerating or proofing dough.

25   Pots -One small one and one large one will do.

26   Pastry brush -A utensil used to spread butter, oil, or glaze. It works well for painting egg wash or cream for a special golden crust and for glazing cakes and cookies.

27   Rolling Pin -For rolling out dough for pies.

28   Rolling pin -A long cylinder with handles used to roll and flatten dough evenly for pies, tarts, and pasta. It's also good for crushing crackers and bread crumbs for press-in crusts and sprinkled-on toppings.

29   Rubber or Silicone Spatula- For scraping batter into or out of a bowl or mixing sticky ingredients.

30   Sifter- A tool that helps you get rid of lumps in dry ingredients like flour.

31   Skewers- Thin metal or wooden sticks used to hold pieces of food together especially while grilling or roasting meats or vegetables.

32   Spatula -A tool with a flat, flexible blade—preferably made of heat-resistant rubber, so you can scrape every last bit out of containers.

33   Tongs -A tool used to grip food. It's great for handling anything you're cooking with precision, whether to turn meat skewers onto the other side while grilling, or rotate carrots in a sauté pan.

34   Vegetable peeler -A tool with a sharp metal blade used to peel the outer layer of sturdy veggies. For more stability, opt for a Y-shaped peeler.

35   Whisk -A handled wire tool used to blend ingredients, smooth and eliminate lumps, and also to emulsify (combine oil and water mixtures together).

36   Whisk- For stirring wet ingredients and incorporating air.

37   Wooden Spoon- For mixing doughs for bread and cookies.

38   Zester or box grater -A device used to grate cheese, zest citrus, grind whole spices like nutmeg and cinnamon, and mince ginger and garlic.

# Basic Cooking Methods

Here are the main stove-top cooking techniques you'll use over and over again:

Dry Heat Cooking

Broiling

Grilling

Roasting

Baking

Sautéing and Pan Frying

Moist Heat Cooking

Poaching

Simmering

Boiling

Steaming

In dry heat cooking, Heat is transferred directly to food without using moisture.

1.    Broiling: Since Broiling is fast, it's beneficial to use a clock or check the desired degree so food doesn't become overcooked. It's a method of transferring extremely high heat onto food. Browning can occur very quickly with this method, sealing juices and flavor inside and leaving a crisp exterior. Best Broiling Foods are: Meats such as steaks, pork chops, or hamburger patties. Poultry such as turkey, breast halves, quarters, and legs. Sturdy fish such as salmon. Fruits like peaches or grapefruit can be broiled.

2.    Grilling: Broiling involves heating from above while Grilling means heating the food from below. In both cases, the food is typically turned once during cooking. Grilling is best for Burger, Meat such as chicken, bones and strip steaks and fish like Salmon, tuna, and swordfish steaks.

3.    Roasting: It is a slow process since heat is passing through the food indirectly and occurs inside an oven at a temperature of 300F. Best Roasting Foods are Meat like Prime rib, beef tenderloin, pork butt and pork loin. Poultry such as chickens or turkeys. Veggies and fruits like Grapes, cherries, tomatoes, Pumpkin, squash, eggplant, and cauliflower.

4.    Baking: In baking as well indirect heat is surrounded with foods and cooks from all sides and is usually performed at lower temperatures than roasting. Best foods for baking are Bread, pastries, cakes and pizzas.

5.    Sautéing: Sautéing is possible using a shallow skillet and a modest quantity of oil. This technique cooks rapidly so it's ideal to keep the food moving by tossing or flipping. To get good results with sautéing, ensure the oiled skillet is hot prior to adding any food; don't stuff too much in oil. Best foods for sautéing are Meats: like ground beef, tenderloin, or medallions. Poultry such as Boneless breasts, strips, or cutlets. Vegetables like Zucchini, squash, and leafy greens, Carrots, celery, and onions.

While moist heat cooking, uses moist or steam to cook food. This in turn provides Healthy dishes, but this will not provide that browned crust for dishes.

1. Poaching: Poaching means submerging food in hot liquid between 140 F and 180 F. The low heat works especially well for delicate items, and moisture and flavor are preserved without the need for fat or oil. Best foods for poaching are Eggs, Poultry like Broth, boneless, skinless chicken breasts. Light Fish: like tilapia, cod, and sole. Fruit like pears or apples for desserts.

2. Simmering: It is also a mild method of cooking foods usually temperature between 180F to 205F. To achieve a simmer, first bring water to the boiling point and then lesser the temperature. Best foods for simmering are Rice, Meats like chuck roast. Soups and Stocks, soups or stews. Root vegetables like potatoes, carrots. Grains like quinoa, oats, or millet.

3. Boiling: Submerging food in water that has been heated to the boiling point of 212F. Once water boils, large bubbles come out, which keep foods in motion while they cook. Best foods for boiling are Pasta, Eggs and Tough root vegetables like potatoes and carrots.

4. Steaming: Water is boiled continuously to produce a steady amount of steam, which makes foods cooked evenly retaining moisture. Best foods for steaming are sturdy veggies like beets, carrots, potatoes, leafy greens. Shellfish like clams, mussels, lobster, or crabs are cooked inside their shells.

# Know Your Knives

Knives are the most common tool used in all recipe preparation. It's useful to know the best uses for various kinds of knives, just as other sharp tools like graters and peelers. To make your work simpler, you need a couple of good blades and sharp tools in your kitchen. There are four sorts of knife that will assist you with your cooking. Utilizing the right knife can make your work simpler.

Safety Tip: Always place a moist cloth or towel under your cutting board to prevent it from sliding while cutting.

1. Chef's knife: An all-purpose knife with a large, sharp, straight-edge blade. It's of finest quality and can be used for chopping, dicing, and slicing food.

2. Butter knife: A small knife with a blunt-edge blade. It's mainly used for slicing soft food or spreading foods such as peanut butter, butter and cream cheese.

3. Paring knife: A sharp small knife, used for peeling and coring food. Also good for finely cutting small amounts of food such as fresh fruits, vegetables, and herbs.

4. Serrated knife: A knife with a sharp saw-like edge. Typically used to slice through bread. Smaller versions can also be used to slice through such food as tomatoes and pineapple.

# How to Ensure Knife Safety

\* Polish knives often. Knife sharpener is an essential tool in kitchen. Sharpening knives prevent chances of knives slipping while cutting and ensure relaxed preparation.

\* Use a cutting board for safe cutting. Don't hold food in your hands while cutting. A cutting board prevents the knife from slipping while cutting and it's connected with the board—not with your skin, ensures safety.

\* Watch your fingers. To prevent injuries, keep your fingers tucked in and concentrate on what you're doing.

\* Carry and store knives correctly. Knives should be stored in a knife rack or knife drawer. Always carry knives by the handle with the tip down and edge facing away from you and others.

\* Keep your knives clean. Take care not to leave knives in the sink or where somebody could get them unexpectedly. Ensure your blades are clean and handles are dry and oil free.

# Using a Knife Carefully

Always get an adult to help you get started with the Knife session and to get familiar with how to hold and use a knife properly.

\* Use both hands while using. Your dominant hand should always hold the knife (If you are a right hander, hold the knife in right hand), while your less dominant hand carefully hold the food in place.

\* Decide what size prior to cutting. Check the recipe to see what needs to be diced, minced, or sliced.

\* Select the correct knife. Prior to starting decide the precise knife and shape.

\* Hold the knife consistent with its size. For smaller blades, fold your fingers over the handle, and place your pointer finger on top of the blade and for bigger blades, fold your fingers over the handle, twisting your pointer finger facing the cutting edge for better control.

\* Observe your fingers while slicing. Tuck in your fingers and place your knuckles against the knife to steer it. Keep your hands and fingers steady to make even slices. Know that dense veggies like carrots can be tough to cut through. Always get an adult assist you while using knife.

# Sharp Tool Uses and Common Cutting Styles

* CHOP- To cut food into small pieces. Chopped food should be uniform in size and may be finely chopped (small pieces) or coarsely chopped (larger pieces), depending on the recipe.

* PEEL -To remove the outer skin/ layer from food, usually a piece of fruit or a vegetable. Often done with a vegetable peeler.

* SLICE -To cut food into thin pieces that are similar thickness dependent on the recipe instructions.

* ZEST- To remove the flavorful colored outer peel from a lemon, lime, or orange (the colored skin is called the zest). Does not include the bitter white layer (called the pith) under the zest.

* MINCE To cut food into very small similar sized pieces and smaller than chopped food.

* GRATE -To cut food (often cheese) into very small, uniform pieces using a rasp grater.

* SHRED -To cut food (often cheese but also some vegetables and fruits) into small, uniform pieces using the large holes on a box grater or the shredding disk of a food processor.

* Dice- To cut food into small cubes. Size may vary but generally from about ¼-inch to ¾-inch in diameter.

* Julienne- To cut food into long thin uniform sized strips, like matchsticks.

# CHAPTER 3:
# TEEN PANTRY

# The Bakers Ingredients and Best Teen Pantry

1. BAKING POWDER -Keep it in dry place with the container tightly closed. Discard any baking powder longer than an year.

2. BAKING SODA- Always mixes this leavening with the other dry ingredients before any liquid is added. Once the dry and liquid ingredients are combined, place the batter in the oven quickly.

3. BUTTER -It brings out a rich, sweet taste in baked goods that nothing else can match. Our recipes use salted butter unless specified otherwise.

4 BUTTERMILK- Use only when specified; it balances sugar's sweetness and reacts with baking soda to give baked goods a fine, crumbly texture.

5. CHOCOLATE -Unsweetened chocolate contains 50–58 percent cocoa butter and no sugar.

6. EGGS -Our recipes require large eggs.

7. EXTRACTS -Use pure, not imitation, extracts whenever possible to obtain the truest flavor. Vanilla is most commonly used, but several of our recipes call for almond extract.

8. SALT -Without salt, sweet baked goods may taste flat. Use table salt for recipes in this book unless otherwise specified.

15. UNSWEETENED COCOA- is a powder made by removing most of the fat from chocolate. Do not substitute instant cocoa mix, as it contains sugar.

## Herbs
Basil
Cilantro
Mint
Parsley
Rosemary
Sage
Nutmeg
Paprika
Peppercorns
Red pepper flakes
Salt (kosher and sea salt)

## Vinegars
Apple cider vinegar
Sherry vinegar
White vinegar
White wine vinegar

## Alliums
Chives
Garlic
Leeks
Onions
Scallions

## Spices
Bay leaves
Cayenne
Chili powder
Cinnamon
Coriander
Cumin
Mustard seeds

## Flour
Whole-wheat flour
All-purpose flour

## Nuts and Seeds
Almonds
Cashews
Flaxseed
Hazelnuts
Pecans
Sesame seeds
Sunflower seeds
Walnuts

## Oils
Coconut oil, raw
Olive oil, extra-virgin
Safflower oil or peanut oil
Sesame oil, toasted

## Fruits and Vegetables
Carrots
Celery
Kale
Lemons
Potatoes
Sweet potatoes
Swiss chard

## Sweeteners
Brown sugar (light and dark varieties)
Cane sugar
Confectioners' sugar
Honey
Maple syrup

## Dairy
Buttermilk
Cheddar
Eggs
Feta
Gruyère
Haloumi
Heavy cream
Parmesan
Ricotta
Whole milk

# CHAPTER 4:
# HEALTHY EASY
# BREAKFAST

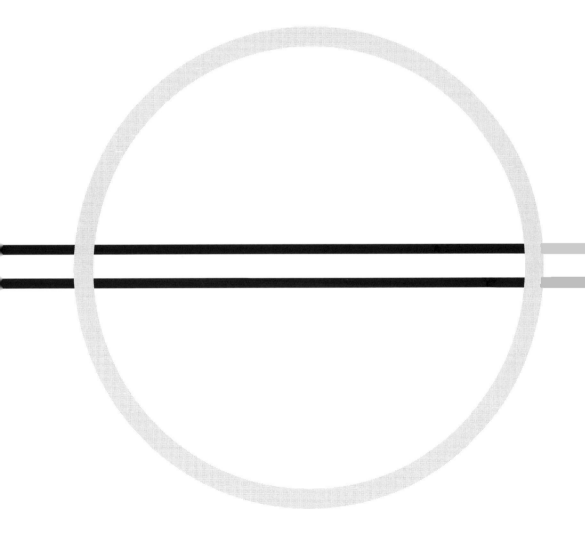

# MUFFINS WITH MARSHMALLOW CREAM

**Prep time: 10 minutes | Cook time: 25 minutes | Makes 12 muffins**

6 large eggs
1 cup milk chocolate chips
1 cup all-purpose flour
1 stick unsalted butter, cut into pieces
1½ cups graham cracker crumbs (from about 15 whole crackers)
2 teaspoons baking powder
½ teaspoon salt
¾ cup sugar
½ cup whole milk
1 teaspoon pure vanilla extract
2 large eggs
¾ cup marshmallow cream

1. Preheat the oven to 350°. Line a 12-cup muffin pan with paper liners. Toss the chocolate chips with 2 teaspoons flour in a small bowl; set aside.

2. Microwave the butter in a separate small microwave-safe bowl until melted. Add the remaining flour, the graham cracker crumbs, baking powder and salt to a large bowl and whisk to combine.

3. Combine the melted butter, sugar, milk, vanilla and eggs in a medium bowl and whisk until smooth.

4. Add the butter mixture to the flour mixture and stir with a rubber spatula until just combined. Add the chocolate chip mixture and stir with the spatula.

5. Pour the batter into the muffin cups with a small ladle or measuring cup, filling those three-quarters of the way. Tap the bottom of the pan lightly against the counter to smooth out the batter.

6. Carefully place in the oven and bake until the muffins are lightly browned and a toothpick inserted into the centers comes out clean, 20 to 25 minutes. Remove the pan from the oven with oven mitts and place on it a wire rack to cool for 5 minutes.

7. Remove the muffins from the pan and place on the rack to cool completely. Spoon 1 tablespoon marshmallow cream onto each muffin. Let set 10 minutes.

# YUMMY BREAKFAST BANANA PANCAKES

**Prep time: 10 minutes | Cook time: 25 minutes | Makes 8 pancakes**

4 tablespoons unsalted butter
1½ cups all-purpose flour
3 tablespoons sugar
1½ teaspoons baking powder
½ teaspoon salt
¼ teaspoon baking soda
1 cup plus 2 tablespoons milk
1 large egg
Cooking spray
FOR THE TOPPINGS
4 ounces (113 g) semisweet chocolate
3 tablespoons heavy cream
2 tablespoons honey
1 banana, sliced
Granola, for topping

1. Make the pancakes: Microwave the butter in a small microwave-safe bowl until melted.

2. Combine the flour, sugar, baking powder, salt and baking soda in a medium bowl and whisk to combine. Combine the milk, melted butter and egg in a separate medium bowl and whisk to combine.

3. Add the milk mixture to the flour mixture and whisk until just combined (it's OK if there are some lumps).

4. Heat a large nonstick skillet or griddle over medium-low heat and coat with cooking spray. Pour in ¼ cup of the batter with a ladle or measuring cup for each pancake and cook until bubbly on top and golden on the bottom, about 4 minutes.

5. Flip with a spatula and cook until golden on the other side, about 2 more minutes. Remove the pancakes and place on a plate.

6. Make the toppings: Carefully chop the chocolate with a chef's knife. Combine the chopped chocolate, heavy cream and honey in a small microwave-safe bowl.

7. Microwave 30 seconds, then stir with a spoon. Continue to microwave, stirring every 30 seconds, until the sauce is smooth. Top the pancakes with the banana slices, chocolate sauce and granola.

Tip: You'll know your pancakes are ready to flip when you see bubbles on the batter.

# CINNAMON TOAST WITH MAPLE SYRUP

Prep time: 10 minutes | Cook time: 40 minutes | Makes 12 cups

6 large eggs
¾ cup milk
¼ cup granulated sugar
¼ teaspoon ground cinnamon
Pinch of ground nutmeg
Pinch of salt

12 slices potato bread or country white bread
4 tablespoons unsalted butter
Confectioners' sugar, for topping
Pure maple syrup, for dipping

1. Preheat the oven to 375°F(191°C). Line a baking sheet with parchment paper. Put the sausages on the baking sheet and bake until lightly browned and cooked through, about 10 minutes.

2. Remove the pan from the oven with oven mitts and let cool slightly.

3. Meanwhile, combine the eggs, milk, granulated sugar, cinnamon, nutmeg and salt in a large bowl and whisk to combine. Cut each slice of bread into a 2-by-4-inch rectangle with a chef's knife, cutting off the crusts, then press the bread gently with your fingertips to flatten slightly.

4. Starting at a short end, roll each piece of bread around a sausage link, pressing firmly with your fingers to seal the seam. Add the bread-wrapped sausages to the bowl with the egg mixture and let soak for 5 minutes.

5. Melt 2 tablespoons butter in a large nonstick skillet over medium heat. Remove 6 of the bread-wrapped sausages from the egg mixture, letting the excess egg drip back into the bowl, then add to the skillet. Cook, turning occasionally with a spatula, until golden brown, about 5 minutes.

6. Carefully remove the pigs in a blanket to paper towels using the spatula. Bunch up a paper towel and hold it with tongs to wipe out the skillet.

7. Add the remaining 2 tablespoons butter to the skillet and repeat with the other 6 bread-wrapped sausages.

8. Sprinkle the confectioners' sugar over the wrapped pigs in a blanket. Serve with maple syrup for dipping.

Pick a Filling

9. Place ½ cup of one of the following ingredients in a medium bowl.

10. Softened cream cheese Mashed banana Ricotta cheese Marshmallow cream

**Add Mix-Ins**

11. Stir in ¼ cup total of the following ingredients (choose 1 or 2).

12. Stuff the Bread

13. Carefully cut four 1½-inch-thick slices from a loaf of challah bread with a serrated knife. With the bread slices flat on a cutting board, carefully cut a 2- to 3-inch-wide slit into the bottom edge of each bread slice with a paring knife to create a deep pocket . Put the filling in a resealable plastic bag and snip a corner. Pipe some filling into each pocket .

Make the Custard

14. Combine 2 eggs, 1 cup half-and-half, 1 tablespoon granulated sugar, 1 teaspoon vanilla, ½ teaspoon ground cinnamon, ¼ teaspoon ground nutmeg and a pinch of salt in a shallow bowl and whisk until combined.

Cook the French Toast

15. Preheat the oven to 250°. Dip a stuffed bread slice in the custard and soak 20 seconds per side; let the excess drip off and place on a plate. Repeat with the remaining bread slices.

16. Heat a large nonstick skillet over medium heat. Melt 1 tablespoon butter in the skillet, then add 2 stuffed bread slices and cook until browned, 4 to 5 minutes per side.

17. Place on a baking sheet and keep warm in the oven. Bunch up a paper towel and hold it with tongs to wipe out the skillet.

18. Repeat with more butter and the other 2 stuffed bread slices. Serve with maple syrup.

# WAFFLES WITH BUTTER AND MAPLE

Prep time: 10 minutes | Cook time: 20 minutes | Makes 12 waffles

5 tablespoons vegetable shortening
4 tablespoons unsalted butter, plus more for topping
2 cups all-purpose flour
4 teaspoons baking powder

2 tablespoons sugar
1 teaspoon salt
2 large eggs
1½ cups milk
Cooking spray
Pure maple syrup, for topping

1. Microwave the shortening and butter in separate small microwave-safe bowls until melted.

2. Combine the flour, baking powder, sugar and salt in a large bowl and whisk to combine. Add the eggs, milk, melted shortening and melted butter and whisk until just combined (it's OK if there are some lumps).

3. Preheat a waffle iron and coat with cooking spray. Slowly pour ⅓ to ½ cup batter into the hot waffle iron with a ladle or measuring cup (the batter should be about 1 inch from the edge of the iron).

4. Close the waffle iron and cook until the waffles are crisp. Carefully remove the waffles with a rubber spatula or tongs and place them on a wire rack to cool. Repeat with the remaining batter to make more waffles.

5. Serve the waffles with butter and maple syrup.

Tip: Keep your leftover waffles to eat as toaster waffles: Just cool them on a wire rack freeze in resealable plastic bags and pop into a toaster for a quick breakfast!

# MUFFINS TOPPED WITH JELLY

**Prep time: 10 minutes | Cook time: 35 minutes | Makes 12 muffins**

6 tablespoons unsalted butter, cut into pieces
⅔ cup whole-wheat flour
⅔ cup all-purpose flour
1 tablespoon baking powder
½ teaspoon salt
⅓ cup creamy peanut butter
1 cup whole milk
½ cup packed light brown sugar
1 teaspoon pure vanilla extract
2 large eggs
FOR THE TOPPINGS
⅔ cup creamy peanut butter
¾ cup honey-roasted peanuts
1 cup strawberry or grape jelly or jam

1. Make the muffins: Preheat the oven to 350°. Line a 12-cup muffin pan with paper liners.

2. Microwave the butter in a small microwave-safe bowl until melted. Add the whole-wheat flour, all-purpose flour, baking powder and salt to a large bowl and whisk to combine.

3. Combine the melted butter, peanut butter, milk, brown sugar, vanilla and eggs in a medium bowl and whisk until smooth. Add the peanut butter mixture to the flour mixture and stir with a rubber spatula until just combined.

4. Pour the batter into the muffin cups with a small ladle or measuring cup, filling those three-quarters of the way.

5. Tap the bottom of the pan lightly against the counter to smooth out the batter. Carefully place in the oven and bake until the muffins are lightly browned and a toothpick inserted into the centers comes out clean, about 25 minutes.

6. Remove the pan from the oven with oven mitts and place it on a wire rack to cool for 5 minutes. Remove the muffins from the pan and place on the rack to cool completely.

7. Make the toppings: Using a teaspoon, scoop out a shallow hole in the middle of each muffin. Microwave the peanut butter in a small microwave-safe bowl, stirring with a spoon halfway through, until loose, 45 to 60 seconds.

8. Finely chop the peanuts with a chef's knife and spread on a plate. Dip the top of a muffin in the melted peanut butter, letting the excess drip off, and then dip it in the chopped peanuts to coat.

9. Place on the rack and repeat with the remaining muffins.

10. Spoon 1 heaping tablespoon jelly or jam into the hole in each muffin. Let sit 5 minutes.

# GOLDEN GERMAN PANCAKE

**Prep time: 5 minutes | Cook time: 15 minutes | serves 4**

¾ cup all-purpose flour
¾ cup whole milk
4 eggs, lightly beaten
2 tablespoons cane sugar
Pinch freshly grated nutmeg
¼ teaspoon sea salt
4 tablespoons butter, divided into 4 pats
Confectioners' sugar, for dusting
Lemon wedges, for serving
Delicious additions
Jam
Cinnamon sugar
Fresh berries
Stewed apples
Whipped cream or crème fraîche
TOOLS / EQUIPMENT
Small, shallow ramekins
Baking sheet
Blender

1. Preheat the oven to 425°F(218°C). Prep the ramekins.

2. Arrange the ramekins on a rimmed baking sheet, and place in the oven to heat.

Blend the ingredients.

3. In a blender, mix the flour, milk, eggs, sugar, nutmeg, and salt until frothy.

4. Butter the ramekins. When the ramekins are hot, add a pat of butter to each and, using pot holders for protection, swirl to coat. Butter should foam. Replace in oven until fully melted.

5. Bake the Dutch Babies. Remove baking sheet from the oven. Divide the batter evenly among the ramekins, and bake until the Dutch Babies are puffed and golden brown, 10 to 15 minutes.

6. Serve.

# WAFFLE EGG SKILLET

**Prep time: 10 minutes | Cook time: 15 minutes | Makes 1 waffle**

1 frozen waffle, thawed but not toasted
1 large egg
1 tablespoon unsalted butter

Kosher salt and freshly ground pepper, to taste
Pure maple syrup, for topping

1. Preheat the oven to 375°. Cut out a 2-inch hole from the center of the waffle with a cookie cutter or small drinking glass.
2. Crack the egg into a small bowl or ramekin. Melt the butter in a small ovenproof nonstick skillet over medium heat.
3. Add the waffle and cook until toasted on the bottom, 2 to 3 minutes. Flip with a spatula. Carefully pour the egg into the hole in the waffle and season with salt and pepper.
4. Cook until the egg white starts to set, about 2 minutes.
5. Carefully put the skillet in the oven and bake until the egg white is set but the yolk is still a little runny, about 4 minutes.
6. Remove the skillet from the oven with oven mitts and remove the waffle to a plate with the spatula. Top with maple syrup.

# DOUGHNUT EGG SKILLET

**Prep time: 10 minutes | Cook time: 15 minutes | Makes 1 doughnut**

1 large egg
1 tablespoon unsalted butter
1 glazed doughnut

Kosher salt and freshly ground pepper, to taste

1. Preheat the oven to 375°. Crack the egg into a small bowl or ramekin. Melt the butter in a small ovenproof nonstick skillet over medium heat.
2. Add the doughnut and cook until toasted on the bottom, 2 to 3 minutes.
3. Flip with a spatula. Carefully pour the egg into the hole in the doughnut; season with salt and pepper. Cook until the egg white starts to set, about 2 minutes.
4. Carefully put the skillet in the oven and bake until the egg white is set but the yolk is still a little runny, about 4 minutes
5. Remove the skillet from the oven with oven mitts and remove the doughnut to a plate with the spatula.

# QUICK AND EASY PEPPERY EGGS

**Prep time: 5 minutes | Cook time: 10 minutes | serves 4**

6 to 8 eggs
Kosher salt, to taste
Freshly ground black pepper, to taste
4 tablespoons butter
Flake salt, such as Maldon, for finishing
Sautéed broccoli or mushrooms
Shredded cheese, folded in or

finely shredded to top
Minced scallions or chives
Diced tomatoes
Bacon or ham
TOOLS / EQUIPMENT
Small bowl
Whisk
Medium sauté pan
Heat-tolerant rubber spatula

1. Beat the eggs. Crack the eggs into a small bowl, and whisk until frothy. Season with salt and pepper.
2. Add the eggs to the pan.
3. Melt the butter in a medium sauté pan over medium heat, and then turn the heat to low as the butter foams. Pour the eggs in and let sit for a few seconds.
4. Cook the eggs. Use a spatula to nudge and stir the eggs, scraping the bottom continuously as you move them around the pan to help prevent sticking.
5. Use the spatula to push the eggs from center-out, and then scrape the pan edge, swirling the outermost eggs into the center.
6. Keep doing this until the eggs begin to look like pudding and then form into dense, rich egg curds, about 4 minutes.
7. Remove the pan from the heat while the eggs are still a little loose; they will continue to cook on the way from the pan to your plate. Sprinkle with a little flake salt and pepper, and eat at once.

# GREEN EGG SANDWICH

**Prep time: 5 minutes | Cook time: 10 minutes | serves 4**

Olive oil, for drizzling and frying
1 baguette or other crusty bread,
sliced into
 5-inch sections and halved
horizontally
⅔ cup grated sharp Cheddar
cheese, divided
 4 eggs
1 handful greens (arugula or
spinach) per
person, rinsed and patted dry
Sea salt, to taste
Freshly ground black pepper, to
taste
TOOLS / EQUIPMENT
Bread knife
Box grater
Toaster oven
Small cast-iron skillet
Metal spatula

1.  Toast the bread. Drizzle a little olive oil onto the cut sides of the bread, and lay the slices on a toaster tray.

2.  Toast until golden and crispy, about 3 minutes. Turn the slices cut-side up, transfer to plates, and sprinkle the cheese evenly on the toast.

3.  Melt the cheese. Return the bread to the toaster oven and broil until the cheese bubbles, about 5 minutes. Carefully transfer the toast to the plates.

4.  Fry the eggs. In a small cast-iron skillet over medium-high heat, fry the eggs in enough olive oil to coat the pan once it is hot. Turn the heat to medium after 1 minute, allowing the whites to cook fully while keeping the yolks soft. Season with salt and pepper.

5.  Serve. Pile the greens onto the toast sandwich bottoms, followed by the fried egg; then top with broiled cheesy toast.

6.  Eat at once, with a plate underneath to catch any drips of liquidy golden

# HEALTHY TORTILLA BAR

**Prep time: 10 minutes | Cook time: 12 minutes | serves 12**

4 to 8 whole-grain (8- or 10-
inch) tortillas
6 to 8 eggs, scrambled
2 cups canned black beans,
drained and rinsed
3 strips cooked bacon,
crumbled
1 cup Greek yogurt or sour
cream
1 cup bite-size cilantro sprigs
1½ cups Salsa Fresca
½ cup orange, red, or green bell
peppers, diced
1½ cups shredded sharp
Cheddar or Monterey Jack
cheese
1½ cups diced avocado or No-
Nonsense Guacamole
Sriracha or Cholula hot sauce,
for garnish
TOOLS / EQUIPMENT
Different-size
Festive bowls
Dish towel
Box grater

Colander
Sauté pan
Aluminum foil

1.  Preheat the oven to 375°F(191°C).Warm the tortillas.

2.  Wrap a stack of 4 tortillas in aluminum foil and warm for 5 to 10 minutes. If you are preparing 8 tortillas, make 2 wrapped bundles. Wrap the warmed foil bundles in a dish towel to keep them toasty.

3.  Serve the fillings and toppings in festive, colorful bowls.

4.  Arrange them together on the table or counter, along with the towel-wrapped tortillas, and allow your guests to assemble their own burrito creations.

# TOMATO-EGG SKILLET WITH BREAD

### Prep time: 10 minutes | Cook time: 20 minutes | serves 4

1 onion, chopped
2 tablespoons olive oil
2 garlic cloves, chopped
1 (28-ounce) can tomatoes or
Homemade Tomato Sauce
1 tablespoon za'atar
2 teaspoons cumin seeds,
toasted and ground in a mortar
and pestle
Kosher salt and freshly ground
black pepper, to taste
4 eggs
¼ cup fresh cilantro leaves, for
garnish

⅔ cup Greek yogurt or sour
cream
Crusty bread, torn, for serving
Delicious additions
Chickpeas
Artichoke hearts
Feta
TOOLS / EQUIPMENT
Toaster oven
Mortar and pestle
Large
Enameled skillet
Wooden spoon

1.  Preheat the oven to 375°F(191°C). Cook the onion and garlic.

2.  In a large enameled skillet over medium heat, sauté the onion in olive oil for 3 to 5 minutes. Add the chopped garlic, and cook for another minute.

3.  Add the tomatoes and aromatics. Add the tomatoes, and bring to a simmer. Add the za'atar and cumin, season with salt and pepper, and simmer uncovered for a few minutes, until the sauce thickens.

4.  Break the tomatoes into chunks using the edge of a wooden spoon. Taste and adjust seasoning as needed.

5.  Add the eggs. Use the wooden spoon to make four nests in the sauce and crack an egg into each. Season the eggs with salt and pepper, and transfer the skillet to the oven, cooking for 7 to 10 minutes, or until the eggs are just set.

6.  Serve from the skillet on a trivet at the table. Season with salt and pepper to taste, and garnish with fresh cilantro and a few dollops of yogurt. Serve with the bread to mop up the sauce and yolks.

# CITRUSY CINNAMON TOAST WITH BUTTER

### Prep time: 10 minutes | Cook time: 20 minutes | serves 4

5 eggs
1⅓ cup whole milk
2 tablespoons fresh-squeezed
orange juice
Zest of 1 orange
1 teaspoon ground cinnamon
Sea salt, to taste
1 tablespoon butter, plus more
as needed for
the pan and for serving
1 tablespoon grape seed oil,

plus more as needed
8 (½-inch-thick) slices brioche
or challah bread
Maple syrup, for serving
TOOLS / EQUIPMENT
Citrus reamer
Zester
Shallow
baking dish
Large cast-iron skillet
Metal spatula

1.  Whisk the ingredients. In a shallow baking dish, use a fork to beat together the eggs, milk, juice, zest, cinnamon, and a large pinch of salt.

2.  Prepare to cook the French toast.

3.  In a large cast-iron skillet over medium heat, heat the butter and grapeseed oil.

4.  Dip the brioche one slice at a time into the egg mixture to coat, puncturing it a couple of times with a fork. Don't let the bread sit in the custard for very long, as it will become soggy.

5.  Pan fry in batches.

6.  When the butter foams, carefully place the bread into the skillet, two slices at a time. Pan fry the bread in batches until golden brown on both sides, flipping when one side is done, about 5 minutes per batch. Repeat with the remaining slices, adding more butter and oil to the pan as needed.

7.  Serve the French toast warm with butter and maple syrup.

# HONEYED MANGO SMOOTHIE

Prep time: 5 minutes | Cook time: 0 minutes | serves 2

2 cups frozen mango chunks
½ bananas
¾ cup whole milk
1 teaspoon honey
1 cup ice
TOOLS/EQUIPMENT
Blender

1. Blend and enjoy. In a blender, combine all the ingredients. Blend until smooth.
2. Pour into 2 glasses and enjoy.

# CHEESY TOMATO FRITTATA

Prep time: 10 minutes | Cook time: 5 minutes | Makes 1 frittata

2 large eggs
1 tablespoon milk
¼ cup shredded mozzarella cheese
2 tablespoons chopped tomato
Kosher salt and freshly ground pepper,
to taste

1. Combine the eggs and milk in a microwave-safe mug and lightly beat with a fork.
2. Add the cheese and tomato, season with salt and pepper and stir until combined.
3. Microwave, stirring every 20 seconds with a spoon, until the eggs are just set, about 1 minute.

# YUMMY WAFFLEWICH WITH MAPLE SYRUP

Prep time: 10 minutes | Cook time: 20 minutes | Makes 1 Wafflewich

2 slices bacon
2 slices cheddar cheese
2 frozen waffles, thawed but not toasted
1 tablespoon unsalted butter
Pure maple syrup, for serving

1. Lay the bacon in a medium skillet and cook over medium-high heat, turning occasionally with tongs or a spatula, until the bacon is crisp, about 8 minutes.
2. Remove the bacon with the tongs or spatula and place on paper towels to drain. Remove the skillet from the heat. Bunch up another paper towel and hold it with tongs to wipe out the skillet.
3. Place 1 slices of cheese on a waffle. Top with the bacon, the other slice of cheese and the other waffle to make a sandwich.
4. Melt the butter in the skillet over medium-low heat.
5. Add the waffle sandwich and cook, flipping with a spatula, until golden and the cheese melts, 3 to 5 minutes per side. Remove to a plate and serve with maple syrup.

# HONEYED GRANOLA

Prep time: 10 minutes | Cook time: 0 minutes | serves 4

24 ounces (680 g) vanilla Greek yogurt`
2 cups granola
2 tablespoons honey
2 cups of your favorite fruits, such as berries or chopped pineapple, kiwi, peaches, etc.
TOOLS/EQUIPMENT
Cutting board (if needed)
Knife (if needed)
4 large glass jars, mugs, or stem less wine glasses

1. Layer the ingredients and serve. Into each of 4 glasses, spoon a layer of yogurt, then a layer of granola.
2. Drizzle the granola layer with a little honey.
3. Top that layer with a layer of fruit. Repeat. Top with another drizzle of honey and enjoy.
`

# HONEYED SESAME PEANUT BAR

**Prep time: 10 minutes | Cook time: 25 minutes | makes 16 bars**

Butter, for greasing
1¼ cups white and/or black sesame seeds
¾ cup unsweetened shredded coconut
½ cup dried apricots, chopped
¼ teaspoon sea salt
¼ cup honey
⅓ cup crunchy peanut butter

¼ teaspoon pure vanilla extract
TOOLS / EQUIPMENT
8-inch-square
glass baking dish
Parchment paper
Large bowl
Small bowl
Rubber spatula
Wire cooling rack

1. Preheat the oven to 350°F(177°C). Prep the baking dish.

2. Butter an 8-inch-square glass baking dish, and line it with parchment paper long enough so that it extends beyond the dish by at least 2 inches on all sides. Cut slits at the corners so the parchment lays flat.

3. Mix the ingredients. In a large bowl, mix together the sesame seeds, coconut, apricots, and salt. In a small bowl, stir the honey, peanut butter, and vanilla extract. Add the honey mixture to the seed-and-fruit mixture, and stir well to combine.

4. Transfer the ingredients and bake.

5. Use a rubber spatula to scrape the mixture into the prepared baking dish, using the broad side of the spatula to press everything into an even layer. Bake until golden around the edges, 20 to 25 minutes. Transfer the baking dish to a wire cooling rack and let cool until firm, about 30 minutes.

6. Serve. Use the parchment tabs to lift the seeded block out of the baking dish—if it starts to crumble, let it cool longer. Using a sharp knife, cut 16 bars. Eat the fruit-seed-nut bars at room temperature. Store any leftovers in a sealed container at room temperature for up to 5 days.

# SAUTÉED EGGS WITH PEPPER

**Prep time: 10 minutes | Cook time: 10 minutes | serves 4**

8 large eggs
1 jalapeño pepper, or less if desired
¼ cup minced onion
1 small tomato
1 tablespoon olive oil
Salt and Freshly ground black pepper, to taste

TOOLS/EQUIPMENT
Cutting board
Knife
1 medium bowl and 1 small bowl
Whisk
Small spoon
Large sauté pan
Spatula

1. Whisk the eggs. Crack the eggs into a medium bowl. Whisk them until frothy, and set aside.

2. Chop the jalapeño.

3. Decide whether to use the whole jalapeño or half, depending on how spicy you like it. Cut the sides of the jalapeño, leaving the stem and seeds to throw away.

4. Scrape off any remaining seeds. Chop the jalapeño, and scrape into a small bowl with the onion.

5. Dice the tomato.

6. Core the tomato by cutting around the tomato core. Discard the core. Scrape out the seeds and juicy pulp with a small spoon. Dice the tomato and add to the bowl with the jalapeño.

7. Cook the ingredients and serve.

8. In a large sauté pan over medium-high heat, heat the oil. Add the jalapeño, tomato, and onion and cook, stirring occasionally, until tender, about 5 minutes. Turn the heat down to low, add the eggs, and cook, folding the eggs over occasionally with a spatula.

9. Season with salt and pepper. Cook for about 4 minutes, or until done to your liking, and serve.

# ALMOND MILK BLUEBERRY SMOOTHIE

**Prep time: 5 minutes | Cook time: 0 minutes | serves 4**

1½ cups nonfat Greek yogurt
2 cups frozen blueberries
1 banana, cut into chunks, or 2 tablespoons honey
3 tablespoons flax meal
¼ cup almond milk or whole milk
Ice, as desired
TOOLS / EQUIPMENT
Blender
Rubber spatula

1. Purée the ingredients: Spoon the yogurt into the blender, followed by the berries, banana, and flax meal.
2. Purée until smooth, adding milk to thin the consistency slightly and ice as desired to keep it slushy. Stop the blender to scrape the sides down as needed.
3. Serve. Pour into glasses and drink chilled.

# PEANUT BUTTER CHIA SEED BOWL

**Prep time: 10 minutes | Cook time: 0 minutes | serves 4**

2 cups Greek yogurt
4 tablespoons flax meal
2 tablespoons chia seeds
4 tablespoons peanut butter
3 cups fresh fruit, such as pomegranate seeds, blueberries, raspberries, or chopped apples, persimmon, or pears
½ cup unsweetened coconut flakes, toasted
2 tablespoons nuts, toasted and coarsely chopped, such as almonds or pistachios
(see Colorful Crunch Salad recipe, here)
TOOLS / EQUIPMENT
Toaster oven

1. Assemble the breakfast bowls and serve.
2. Stir the yogurt until creamy. Divide the yogurt evenly into bowls. Sprinkle the flax meal and chia seeds evenly into each.
3. Spoon the peanut butter on top, then the fruit. Scatter the toasted coconut and chopped nuts to finish each bowl, and eat immediately.

# SWEET AND CITRUSY FRUIT SALAD

**Prep time: 10 minutes | Cook time: 0 minutes | serves 4**

1 cup strawberries, halved
1 cup blueberries
1 cup grapes, halved
Zest of ½ lime
2 tablespoons freshly squeezed lime juice
2 tablespoons honey (more to taste if you want it sweeter)
TOOLS/EQUIPMENT
Cutting board
Knife
Microplane or zester
Serving bowl

1. Mix the fruit. In a serving bowl, toss together the strawberries, blueberries, and grapes.
2. Flavor and serve. Sprinkle the lime zest onto the fruit, toss with the lime juice, and serve.

# DELICIOUS THYME HERBED PORK

**Prep time: 10 minutes | Cook time: 6 minutes | serves 6**

2 pounds ground pork
1 tablespoon maple syrup
1½ teaspoons kosher salt
1 teaspoon freshly ground black pepper
⅛ teaspoon red pepper flakes
2 garlic cloves, minced, or 2 tablespoons garlic paste
1 tablespoon chopped fresh sage
1 teaspoon chopped fresh thyme
1 tablespoon olive oil or grapeseed oil
TOOLS/EQUIPMENT
Cutting board
Knife
Large bowl
Large nonstick frying pan or sauté pan
Plastic or silicone spatula

1. Form the patties. In a large bowl, combine all the ingredients except the oil. Mix with your hands until fully blended. Cover and refrigerate for 15 to 30 minutes. Form into patties.
2. Brown the sausage and serve.
3. In a large nonstick pan over medium-high heat, heat the oil (use more if needed). Cook the patties, allowing a little room between them, for 2½ to 3 minutes per side, or until browned and cooked through, and serve.

# CINNAMON SPICED QUINOA BOWL

### Prep time: 10 minutes | Cook time: 5minutes | serves 4

1 cup red or golden quinoa
2 cups almond or cashew milk, plus more for drizzling
½ teaspoon ground cinnamon
¼ teaspoon freshly grated nutmeg
¾ cup fresh or frozen blueberries
Pinch kosher salt
2 bananas

Maple syrup, for serving
TOOLS / EQUIPMENT
Medium glass
Bowl with lid
Fine grater
Medium saucepan
Heat-tolerant
Rubber spatula

1. Soak the quinoa overnight. Transfer the quinoa to a glass bowl or container with a lid.

2. Add the nut milk, cinnamon, and nutmeg. Soak on the counter overnight, lid slightly askew.

3. The next morning, heat the quinoa. In a medium saucepan over medium-low heat, add the frozen berries and a pinch of salt to the quinoa mixture and warm, about 5 minutes.

4. Have a few tablespoons of water or more nut milk nearby to drizzle in case the quinoa sticks as you stir. If using fresh berries, add them when the porridge is almost warm enough to eat.

5. Serve. Spoon the quinoa into bowls, and slice bananas on top. If you like, add more freshly grated nutmeg and a dash of cinnamon. At the table, drizzle maple syrup over the top and eat at once.

# MAPLE DRIZZLED OATMEAL

### Prep time: 10 minutes | Cook time: 30 minutes | serves 6

2 cups old-fashioned oats
2 teaspoons ground cinnamon or apple pie spice
Pinch salt
1 heaping cup peeled, diced Granny Smith apples
¾ cup Cinnamon Applesauce or apple butter
¼ cup whole milk
¼ cup grape seed or olive oil
2 large eggs

3 tablespoons maple syrup, plus more for drizzling
TOOLS/EQUIPMENT
Cutting board
Knife
Peeler
8-by-8-inch baking dish
Large bowl
Mixing spoon
Nonstick cooking spray

1. Preheat the oven. Preheat the oven to 350°F(177°C). Spray an 8-by-8-inch baking dish with cooking spray, and set aside.

2. Mix the ingredients. In a large bowl, combine all the ingredients and stir until fully blended.

3. Bake the oatmeal and serve. Scrape the batter into the prepared baking dish and spread evenly. Bake for 30 minutes, or until golden brown on top.

4. Allow to sit for 5 minutes before serving. Drizzle with additional maple syrup if desired, and enjoy!

# CHEESY BREAD WITH BAKED EGG

Prep time: 10 minutes | Cook time: 20 minutes | serves 4

1 loaf ciabatta bread or French bread
4 to 6 large eggs
2 to 3 tablespoons heavy or light cream,
divided
1 tablespoon chopped fresh parsley
1 tablespoon chopped scallion
Salt and Freshly ground black pepper, to taste
2 to 3 tablespoons shredded Parmesan or Cheddar cheese
TOOLS/EQUIPMENT
Cutting board
Knife
Baking sheet

1. Preheat the oven. Preheat the oven to 350°F(177°C). Assemble the loaf.

2. Set the bread on a baking sheet. Depending on the size of your bread loaf, cut 4 to 6 circles in the top ½ inch or so apart and about 2 inches in diameter. Scoop out the bread from the circles about an inch deep to form holes.

3. Fill the holes. Crack an egg into each hole, top each with ½ tablespoon of cream and some parsley, scallions, salt, and pepper. Sprinkle with the cheese.

4. Bake and serve. Bake for 20 minutes, or until the eggs are done to your liking. Cut into equal size pieces and serve.

# EASY CHEESY BROCCOLI PIE

Prep time: 10 minutes | Cook time: 50 minutes | serves 6

1 frozen deep-dish piecrust
1½ cups whole milk
3 large eggs
1 tablespoon flour
1 tablespoon melted butter
Dash salt
Dash freshly ground black pepper
½ cup diced broccoli (frozen and thawed works best)
6 ounces (170 g) shredded Cheddar cheese
TOOLS/EQUIPMENT
Grater
Deep-dish pie pan (if needed)
Rimmed baking sheet
Large bowl
Whisk
Mixing spoon
Knife

1. Preheat the oven. Preheat the oven to 375°F(191°C).

2. Prepare the crust. If your pie dough is not already in a disposable pie tin, press it into a deep-dish pie pan. Place the dough-filled pie pan on a rimmed baking sheet.

3. Mix the ingredients. In a large bowl, whisk together the milk, eggs, flour, butter, salt, and pepper until combined. Stir in the broccoli and cheese.

4. Pour, bake, and serve. Pour the mixture into the pie pan, being careful not to overfill past three-quarters full.

5. Place the pie on the rimmed baking sheet in the oven, and bake for 45 to 50 minutes, or until the quiche is puffed up and golden brown on top. Once removed from the oven, allow the quiche to set for at least 10 minutes before slicing and serving.

# CRISPY BACON WITH POTATOES

Prep time: 10 minutes | Cook time: 20 minutes | serves 6

4 russet potatoes
½ pound bacon
1 large red or green pepper, diced
1 medium sweet onion, diced
Freshly ground black pepper, to taste
Pinch salt
TOOLS/EQUIPMENT

Cutting board
Paring or chef's knife
Microwave-safe dish
Kitchen shears (optional)
Large skillet
Slotted spoon
Spatula
Paper towel
Plate

1. Prep the potatoes. Scrub the potatoes, removing dirt and debris. Cut the potatoes into even, bite-size chunks.

2. Place in a microwave-safe dish, partially covered, and microwave for 3 minutes. Allow the potatoes to cool.

3. Cook the bacon.

4. Meanwhile, using kitchen shears or a knife, cut the bacon into 1-inch pieces. In a large skillet over medium heat, carefully sauté on both sides until just crisp, about 8 minutes. Using a slotted spoon or spatula, transfer the bacon to a paper towel–lined plate, reserving the bacon fat in the pan.

5. Cook the veggies and serve.

6. Add the peppers and onion to the pan with the hot bacon fat. Cook over medium heat, stirring occasionally, for 3 minutes, or until the peppers are tender.

7. Add the potatoes, season well with pepper and a pinch of salt (the bacon drippings are already salty), and continue cooking until the potatoes crisp up a bit, about 4 minutes.

8. Add the crispy bacon pieces, toss, and serve.

# BLUEBERRY PANCAKE WITH BERRY COMPOTE

Prep time: 10 minutes | Cook time: 10 minutes | serves 4

FOR THE PANCAKES
1½ cups flour
2 tablespoons sugar
2 teaspoons baking powder
½ teaspoon baking soda
Pinch salt
1 large egg
1½ cups buttermilk
1½ tablespoons melted butter
1 pint blueberries
FOR THE COMPOTE
1 pint strawberries, hulled and quartered
¼ cup granulated sugar
3 tablespoons water

½ tablespoon fresh squeezed lemon juice
Powdered sugar, for sprinkling
TOOLS/EQUIPMENT
Cutting board
Knife
1 medium bowl and 1 small bowl
Whisk
Large, nonstick skillet
Ice cream scoop or ⅓ cup measuring cup
Spatula
Small pot
Small mesh strainer

1. Mix the dry ingredients. In a medium bowl, combine the flour, sugar, baking powder, baking soda, and salt, and whisk until all ingredients are incorporated. Set aside.

2. Mix the wet ingredients. In a small bowl, whisk the egg. Add the buttermilk and butter, and whisk until combined.

3. Mix the wet and dry ingredients together.

4. Add the wet ingredients to the dry ingredients, and whisk just until combined. Do not overmix; some lumps are okay. Allow the batter to sit for about 10 minutes.

5. Make the compote. While the batter sits, in a small pot over medium-high heat, combine all the compote ingredients, except the powdered sugar.

Bring to a simmer. After 2 minutes, remove the pot from the heat and allow to cool down. The compote can be made a day ahead and stored in a mason jar or lidded container.

6. Cook the pancakes. When ready to cook, set a large, nonstick skillet over medium-high heat. Use an ice cream scoop or a ⅓ cup measuring cup to scoop the batter and pour it into the pan, making "puddles" of batter. Quickly arrange the blueberries on top. Once bubbles form and pop, flip the pancakes and cook through.

7. Assemble and serve. Use a small mesh strainer to top the pancakes with a nice sprinkle of powdered sugar; add a couple spoonfuls of the berry compote and serve.

# HOMEMADE CHEESY PIZZA

Prep time: 10 minutes | Cook time: 15 minutes | serves 4

Flour, for dusting the pan
1 disk fresh pizza dough, store-bought or from
a pizza shop
Olive oil
Salt and Freshly ground black pepper, to taste
15 asparagus spears, woody ends trimmed
10 slices Virginia ham, torn into pieces
1 cup shredded Monterey Jack cheese
½ cup shredded mozzarella
4 large eggs, each cracked into a separate small
bowl or ramekin
TOOLS/EQUIPMENT
Grater
4 small bowls or ramekins
Pizza stone or baking sheet
Basting brush (or paper towel)
Large bowl
Pizza cutter or knife

1. Prepare the oven. Position an oven rack in the middle of the oven. Prepare a pizza stone or baking sheet by scattering flour lightly onto the surface. Preheat the oven to 450°F(232°C).

2. Prepare the dough. Shape the pizza dough into either a rustic rectangle or a traditional round, depending on the shape of your pan. Brush the dough lightly with oil, and season with salt and pepper.

3. Add the asparagus. Place a small amount of oil in your clean hands. In a large bowl, toss the asparagus spears with your hands, lightly coating them. Season the asparagus with salt and pepper, then arrange the asparagus in a sunburst pattern, with the tips pointing outward.

4. Bake the pizza and eggs and serve. Place in the oven and bake for 5 minutes. Remove from the oven, place ham all over the pizza, top with the cheeses, and slide each egg onto a separate quarter of the pizza.

5. Sprinkle the eggs with salt and pepper, and quickly return the pizza to the oven.

6. Bake for an additional 10 minutes, or until the crust is golden and the eggs are set to your liking. Cool slightly, slice into 4 wedges, and serve.

# SWEET BANANA BUTTER CAKE

Prep time: 10 minutes | Cook time: 50 minutes | serves 6

FOR THE CAKE
Nonstick cooking spray
2 cups all-purpose flour
2½ tablespoons baking powder
½ teaspoon salt
3 overripe bananas
2 cups granulated sugar
1 cup whole milk
½ cup melted and cooled butter
2 large eggs
1 teaspoon vanilla extract
FOR THE CRUMB TOPPING
1½ cups brown sugar
1½ cups all-purpose flour
6 tablespoons cold butter, cut into 12 pieces
TOOLS/EQUIPMENT
Cutting board
Knife
13-by-9-inch baking dish
1 small, 1 large, and 1 medium bowl
Whisk
Potato masher
Pastry cutter (optional)
Toothpick
Preheat the oven.

1. Preheat the oven to 350°F(177°C). Spray a 13-by-9-inch baking dish with cooking spray. Set aside. Mix the dry ingredients.

2. In a small bowl, whisk together the flour, baking powder, and salt. Set aside. Mix the batter.

3. In a large bowl, mash the bananas with a potato masher until mushy. Add the granulated sugar, milk, butter, eggs, and vanilla, and stir until fully combined. Add the flour mixture, and mix until fully combined. Scrape the batter into the prepared baking dish.

4. Add the topping. In a medium bowl, combine the brown sugar, flour, and butter. Using a pastry cutter or your fingertips, blend until the mixture resembles crumbs. Sprinkle the topping over the batter.

5. Bake the cake and serve. Bake for 45 to 50 minutes, or until a toothpick inserted into the middle comes out dry. Allow the cake to cool, then cut into squares and serve.

# SWEET AND CITRUSY BLUEBERRY SCONES

**Prep time: 10 minutes | Cook time: 20 minutes | serves 6**

1½ cups all-purpose flour, plus more for scattering
¼ cup sugar, plus more for sprinkling
½ tablespoon baking powder
⅛ teaspoon salt
6 tablespoons cold butter, cut into 12 pieces
½ cup dried blueberries
½ cup buttermilk, plus more for brushing the dough
½ tablespoon lemon zest
**TOOLS/EQUIPMENT**

Cutting board
Knife
Microplane or zester
Baking sheet
Parchment paper or silicone baking mat
Large bowl
Whisk
Mixing spoon
Pastry cutter (optional)
Chef's knife
Pastry brush
Toothpick

1. Preheat the oven. Preheat the oven to 400°F(204°C). Line a baking sheet with parchment paper or a silicone baking mat

2. Mix the ingredients. In a large bowl, combine the flour, sugar, baking powder, and salt, and whisk together. Using a pastry cutter or your clean fingertips, work the butter into the flour mixture until it resembles pea-size balls.

3. Add the blueberries, stirring to combine. Add the buttermilk and lemon peel, and mix until a dough forms.

4. Prepare the dough. Scatter some flour onto a clean countertop. Transfer the dough to the floured counter, and use your hands to work it until all the flour is mixed in.

5. Shape the dough into a round disk. Break the dough into two pieces and shape into two 1-inch-high disks. Transfer the disks to the prepared baking sheet. Using a chef's knife, cut each disk into 4 to 6 wedges. Space the wedges slightly apart.

6. Bake the scones. Brush the tops of the dough with a bit of buttermilk, and sprinkle with sugar and lemon zest.

7. Bake for 15 to 20 minutes, or until a toothpick inserted into the thickest part comes out mostly clean, and serve.

# BUTTERY PUMPKIN MUFFINS

**Prep time: 10 minutes | Cook time: 10 minutes | serves 6**

**FOR THE MUFFINS**
Nonstick cooking spray
1¾ cups flour
1½ teaspoons baking powder
1½ teaspoons pumpkin pie spice
¼ to ½ cup butter, melted
½ teaspoon salt
1 cup pumpkin purée (not pumpkin pie filling)
¾ cup sugar
⅓ cup vegetable oil
1 large egg

**FOR THE COATING**
⅓ cup sugar
1 tablespoon pumpkin pie spice
¼ to ½ cup butter, melted
**TOOLS/EQUIPMENT**
Mini muffin pan
1 medium bowl, 1 large bowl, and 2 small bowls
Mixing spoon
Toothpick
Parchment paper
Wire rack (optional)

1. Preheat the oven. Preheat the oven to 350°F(177°C), and spray a mini muffin pan with cooking spray.

2. Mix the dry ingredients. In a medium bowl, mix together the flour, baking powder, pumpkin pie spice, and salt. Set aside.

3. Mix the wet ingredients. In a large bowl, combine the pumpkin purée, sugar, oil, and egg. Add the dry ingredients to the wet ingredients, and stir until combined.

4. Bake the muffins. Fill the muffin cups three-quarters full with batter. Bake for 8 to 9 minutes, or until a toothpick inserted into the center of a muffin comes out clean.

5. Prepare the coating. In a small bowl, mix the sugar and pumpkin pie spice. Set this bowl next to your bowl of melted butter.

6. Coat and serve. Transfer the muffins onto parchment paper. While still hot, dip them one by one into the melted butter, then immediately roll in the sugar mixture, coating the muffin entirely. Enjoy hot or place on a wire rack to cool.

# CHAPTER 5: YUMMY LUNCH

# BUTTERY SANDWICH WITH KALE CHIPS

## Prep time: 10 minutes | Cook time: 30 minutes | Makes 4

FOR THE KALE CHIPS
1 bunch Tuscan kale (about 1 pound)
1 tablespoon extra-virgin olive oil
Kosher salt
FOR THE SANDWICHES
1 Granny Smith apple, peeled
and grated on the large holes of a box grater
⅓ cup honey mustard
8 frozen waffles
½ pound sliced deli ham
¼ pound sliced cheddar cheese
2 tablespoons unsalted butter, plus more if needed

1. Make the kale chips: Preheat the oven to 275°. Carefully cut off the tough stems of the kale with a chef's knife; discard.

2. Chop the kale leaves into 1½-inch pieces. Toss the kale on a baking sheet with the olive oil and ½ teaspoon salt and spread in a single layer.

3. Bake the kale for 10 minutes, then remove the baking sheet from the oven with oven mitts and flip the kale leaves with tongs or a spatula. Put back in the oven and continue to bake until the kale leaves are crisp, about 10 more minutes.

4. Meanwhile, make the sandwiches: Stir together the grated apple with the honey mustard in a medium bowl until combined. Spoon the apple mixture on 4 waffles and spread evenly. Top with the ham, cheese and remaining waffles to make 4 sandwiches.

5. Melt the butter in a large nonstick skillet over medium heat. Carefully add the sandwiches and cook, flipping once with a spatula, until golden, about 3 minutes per side.

6. Add more butter to the skillet when you flip the sandwich, if needed. Serve with the kale chips.

# GARLICKY STEAK WITH CHIMICHURRI SAUCE

## Prep time: 15 minutes | Cook time: 10 minutes | serves 4

4 pieces strip steak, rib eye steak, or fillet steaks
½ teaspoon kosher salt, plus more for seasoning the steak
¼ teaspoon freshly ground black pepper, plus more for seasoning the steak
5 garlic cloves, chopped
2 tablespoons fresh oregano leaves
1 teaspoon red pepper flakes
¼ cup chopped fresh parsley
¼ cup chopped fresh cilantro
3 tablespoons red wine vinegar
½ cup grape seed or olive oil, plus more if needed
TOOLS/EQUIPMENT
Cutting board
Knife
Paper towel
Food processor or high-powered blender
Small bowl
Large, heavy skillet or cast-iron pan
Tongs
Meat thermometer
Serving plate

1. Prepare the steaks. Pat the steaks dry with a paper towel. Season well with kosher salt and pepper, and set aside to rest at room temperature for 20 to 30 minutes.

2. Blend the sauce. In a food processor or high-powered blender, combine the garlic, oregano, red pepper flakes, parsley, cilantro, and vinegar.

3. Pulse until the garlic and greens are finely chopped and the sauce is blended. Pour into a small bowl and set aside.

4. Cook the steaks. In a large, heavy skillet or cast-iron pan over medium-high heat, heat the oil. Swirl the oil around to coat the pan. Once the oil begins to shimmer and the first wisp of smoke appears, add the steaks, leaving room in between.

5. Cook for 3 to 5 minutes on one side (see Helpful Hint), then use tongs to turn the steaks over and cook to desire doneness or until a meat thermometer inserted in the thickest part of the steak reads 145°F(63°C), for medium.

6. Add more oil if the pan looks dry. Rest the steaks and serve.

7. Remove the steaks from the pan and allow them to rest for 5 to 10 minutes without touching them.

8. Transfer the steaks to a serving plate, spoon a line of chimichurri sauce down the middle of each, and serve.

## CINNAMON SPICED CHEESY SANDWICH

Prep time: 10 minutes | Cook time: 10 minutes | Makes 1

1 tablespoon cream cheese, at room temperature
1 tablespoon goat cheese, at room temperature
1 teaspoon chopped walnuts
1 teaspoon pure maple syrup
2 slices cinnamon-raisin bread
1 tablespoon unsalted butter, plus more if needed

1. Mix the cream cheese, goat cheese, walnuts and maple syrup in a small bowl with a rubber spatula.
2. Spread the cream cheese mixture on the bread slices and sandwich them together.
3. Melt the butter in a nonstick skillet over medium-low heat. Carefully add the sandwich and cook, flipping once with a spatula, until golden brown and the cheese mixture softens, 2 to 3 minutes per side.
4. Add more butter to the skillet when you flip the sandwich, if needed.

## CHEESY HAM SKILLET

Prep time: 10 minutes | Cook time: 10 minutes | Makes 1

1 croissant
1 tablespoon dijonnaise
2 slices Muenster cheese
1 thin slice deli ham
1 tablespoon unsalted butter, at room temperature

1. Carefully split open the croissant with a serrated knife. Spread the dijonnaise on the cut sides.
2. Layer 1 slice of cheese, the ham and another slice of cheese on the bottom half of the croissant. Cover with the top half of the croissant. Spread the butter all over the outside of the sandwich.
3. Heat a small nonstick skillet over medium-low heat until hot. Carefully add the sandwich and press it down with the bottom of another skillet.
4. Leave the skillet in place and cook the sandwich, flipping it once with a spatula, until golden brown and the cheese melts, about 3 minutes per side.

## DOUBLE CHEESED TOMATO PIZZA

Prep time: 10 minutes | Cook time: 10 minutes | Makes 1

1 tablespoon tomato sauce
2 slices sourdough bread
2 tablespoons shredded mozzarella cheese
1 tablespoon grated parmesan cheese
3 basil leaves
1 tablespoon unsalted butter, plus more if needed

1. Spread the tomato sauce on 1 slice of bread. Top with the mozzarella, parmesan, basil and the other slice of bread.
2. Melt the butter in a small nonstick skillet over medium-low heat. Carefully add the sandwich and cook, flipping it once with a spatula, until golden brown and the cheese melts, 3 to 4 minutes per side.
3. Add more butter to the skillet when you flip the sandwich, if needed.

## EASY CHEESY HOAGIE SANDWICH

Prep time: 10 minutes | Cook time: 10 minutes | Makes 1

1 hoagie roll
2 slices provolone cheese
4 thin slices salami
1 tablespoon chopped hot cherry peppers or roasted red peppers
1 tablespoon extra-virgin olive oil

1. Carefully split the roll in half lengthwise with a serrated knife.
2. Layer 1 slice of cheese, the salami, hot cherry peppers and the other slice of cheese on the bottom half of the roll. Cover with the top half of the roll.
3. Heat the olive oil in a small nonstick skillet over medium-low heat. Carefully add the sandwich and press it down with the bottom of another skillet.
4. Leave the skillet in place and cook the sandwich, flipping it once with a spatula, until golden brown and the cheese melts, 3 to 4 minutes per side.

# SCALLION SANDWICH WITH TOMATO SOUP

**Prep time: 10 minutes | Cook time: 35 minutes | serves 4**

FOR THE SOUP
4½ pounds tomatoes
1½ tablespoons extra-virgin olive oil
1 clove garlic, minced
2 scallions, chopped
1½ tablespoons heavy cream
Kosher salt and freshly ground pepper
½ cup mini bow ties or other mini pasta

Chopped fresh basil, for topping
FOR THE SANDWICHES
½ cup shredded part-skim mozzarella cheese
½ cup shredded sharp cheddar cheese
2 scallions, chopped
4 slices multigrain bread
2 thin slices low-sodium deli ham

½ tablespoon extra-virgin olive oil

1. Make the soup: Carefully cut 4 pounds of the tomatoes into quarters with a serrated knife and chop the rest. Put the quartered tomatoes in a blender and puree until smooth.

2. Heat the olive oil in a large pot over medium heat. Add the garlic and scallions and cook, stirring with a wooden spoon, 2 minutes.

3. Increase the heat to medium high. Hold a fine-mesh sieve over the pot and strain the pureed tomatoes into the pot. Stir in the chopped tomatoes, 1 cup water, the heavy cream, ½ teaspoon salt and ¼ teaspoon pepper. Bring to a simmer and cook until thickened, about 5 minutes.

4. Add the pasta to the soup and cook until tender, about 10 minutes. Season with salt and pepper.

5. Meanwhile, make the sandwiches: Toss the cheeses with the scallions in a medium bowl. Sprinkle half the mixture on 2 slices of bread. Top each with a slice of ham, the remaining cheese mixture and the other 2 slices of bread.

6. Heat the olive oil in a large nonstick skillet over medium-low heat. Carefully add the sandwiches and cook, flipping once with a spatula, until the cheese melts, about 3 minutes per side.

7. Ladle the soup into bowls and top with basil. Serve each bowl with a sandwich half.

Tip: Bruised or imperfect tomatoes are great for making soup. Just be sure your tomatoes aren't rotten: If they're leaking liquid or show signs of mold, you should toss them.

# ENTICING TOMATO BEEF BAKE

**Prep time: 10 minutes | Cook time: 50 minutes | Makes 4**

2 teaspoons vegetable oil, plus more for brushing
1 shallot, finely chopped
1 clove garlic, minced
Pinch of ground cinnamon
½ pound ground beef
Kosher salt and freshly ground pepper, to taste
1 tablespoon tomato paste

3 tablespoons chopped tomato
3 tablespoons golden raisins
3 large pimiento-stuffed olives, finely chopped
All-purpose flour, for dusting
1 11-ounce tube refrigerated French bread dough
1 large egg

1. Heat the vegetable oil in a medium skillet over medium-high heat.

2. Add the shallot, garlic and cinnamon and cook, stirring with a wooden spoon, 1 minute.

3. Add the beef, ¼ teaspoon salt and a few grinds of pepper. Cook, breaking up the meat with the wooden spoon, until browned, about 3 minutes.

4. Add the tomato paste, chopped tomato, raisins and olives to the skillet and cook, stirring to coat, 2 minutes.

5. Season with salt and pepper. Remove from the heat and let the beef mixture cool completely.

6. Preheat the oven to 425° (218°C). Lightly brush a baking sheet with vegetable oil. Lightly dust your work surface with flour.

7. Cut the French bread dough into 4 equal pieces. Using a rolling pin, roll out each piece of dough on the floured surface into a 6-by-8-inch rectangle.

8. Divide the beef mixture among the dough rectangles, piling it in the center. Fold the 2 shorter sides of the dough over the filling, stretching the dough to cover. Fold in the 2 long sides to enclose. Pinch the seams with your fingers to seal.

9. Move the pockets seam-side down to the oiled baking sheet. Beat the egg and 1 tablespoon water with a fork in a small bowl.

10. Brush the pockets with the egg wash. Bake until golden brown, about 15 minutes. Remove from the oven using oven mitts and let cool slightly.

# BROILED MUFFIN WITH SWEET POTATO CHIPS

**Prep time: 10 minutes | Cook time: 10 minutes | serves 1**

> 2 tablespoons mayonnaise
> ½ teaspoon curry powder
> 1 3-ounce can tuna, drained
> 1 scallion, thinly sliced
> Kosher salt and freshly ground
> pepper, to taste
> 1 English muffin, split
> 2 small slices cheddar cheese
> Sweet potato chips, for topping

1. Preheat the broiler. Mix together the mayonnaise and curry powder in a small bowl. Stir in the tuna and scallion. Season with salt and pepper.
2. Toast the English muffin in a toaster. Spread the tuna mixture on the cut sides of the English muffin. Top each half with a slice of cheese.
3. Place the English muffin halves on a baking sheet, carefully place under the broiler and broil until the cheese is melted, about 3 minutes. Top with sweet potato chips.

# CHEESY MUFFIN WITH SALSA

**Prep time: 10 minutes | Cook time: 10 minutes | serves 1**

> 1 English muffin, split
> 2 tablespoons refried beans
> 2 tablespoons shredded
> pepper jack cheese
> Salsa, sour cream, chopped
> pickled jalapeños
> and fresh cilantro, for topping

1. Preheat the broiler. Toast the English muffin in a toaster. Spread the beans on the cut sides of the English muffin and top with the cheese.
2. Place the English muffin halves on a baking sheet, carefully place under the broiler and broil until the cheese is melted, about 3 minutes.
3. Top with salsa, sour cream, pickled jalapeños and cilantro.
Tip: Split English muffins in half with a fork, not a knife, so you'll end up with good nooks and crannies.

# BEAN TORTILLA CUPS WITH SALSA

**Prep time: 10 minutes | Cook time: 10 minutes | Makes 6**

> Cooking spray
> 6 6-inch flour tortillas
> Kosher salt
> Chili powder, to taste
> ¾ cup refried beans
> ¾ cup guacamole
> Sour cream, fresh salsa, cilantro
> and shredded
> lettuce and cheddar, for topping

1. Preheat the oven to 425°. Coat a 6-cup jumbo muffin pan with cooking spray. Press 1 tortilla into each cup, pleating it to make it fit.
2. Lightly coat the tortillas with cooking spray and season each with salt and a pinch of chili powder.
3. Bake the tortilla cups until golden, 8 to 10 minutes. Remove from the oven using oven mitts, place the muffin pan on a rack and let the tortilla cups cool completely.
4. Carefully remove the tortilla cups from the muffin pan. Divide the beans and guacamole among the cups. Top each with sour cream, salsa, cilantro, lettuce and cheese.

# HOMEMADE FRIED RICE WITH SCALLIONS

**Prep time: 10 minutes | Cook time: 10 minutes | serves 4**

> 1 tablespoon sesame oil
> ½ cup chopped sweet onion
> ½ cup frozen peas and carrots
> 1 large egg, lightly beaten
> 1½ cups cooked rice
> 2 tablespoons soy sauce
> 3 tablespoons chopped scallions
> TOOLS/EQUIPMENT
> Cutting board
> Knife
> Large sauté pan or wok
> Spatula
> Serving bowl

1. Cook the veggies. In a large skillet or wok over medium-high heat, heat the oil. Once the oil is hot, add the onion and peas and carrots mixture, and cook for 4 to 5 minutes, or until tender.
2. Scramble the egg. Using a spatula, push the vegetable mixture to the side of the pan.
3. Add the beaten egg, and scramble it in the pan. Once the egg is cooked through, mix the vegetables into the egg.
4. Add the rice, stirring to incorporate. Add the soy sauce, and stir thoroughly, cooking until heated through.
5. Garnish and serve. Transfer the rice to a serving bowl, sprinkle the scallions over top, and serve.

# SPICY CHICKEN PEAS POCKETS

**Prep time: 10 minutes | Cook time: 50 minutes | Makes 4**

1 tablespoon vegetable oil, plus more for brushing
1 shallot, finely chopped
¾ teaspoon curry powder
½ teaspoon grated peeled fresh ginge0072
1 clove garlic, grated
1 cup shredded rotisserie chicken (skin removed)
¼ cup frozen peas, thawed

¼ cup plain low-fat yogurt
2 tablespoons chopped fresh cilantro
1 teaspoon fresh lime juice
Kosher salt, to taste
All-purpose flour, for dusting
1 (11-ounce /311 g) tube refrigerated French bread dough
1 large egg

1. Heat the vegetable oil in a medium skillet over medium heat.
2. Add the shallot, curry powder, ginger and garlic and cook, stirring with a wooden spoon, until the shallot is slightly softened, about 2 minutes. Stir in the chicken. Remove the skillet from the heat.
3. Stir the peas, yogurt, cilantro and lime juice into the chicken mixture. Season with salt. Let the chicken mixture cool completely.
4. Preheat the oven to 425°. Lightly brush a baking sheet with vegetable oil. Lightly dust your work surface with flour. Cut the French bread dough into 4 equal pieces. Using a rolling pin, roll out each piece of dough on the floured surface into a 6-by-8-inch rectangle.
5. Divide the chicken mixture among the dough rectangles, piling it in the center.
6. Fold the 2 shorter sides of the dough over the filling, stretching the dough to cover. Fold in the 2 long sides to enclose. Pinch the seams with your fingers to seal.
7. Move the pockets seam-side down to the oiled baking sheet. Beat the egg and 1 tablespoon water with a fork in a small bowl. Brush the pockets with the egg wash.
8. Bake until golden brown, about 15 minutes. Remove from the oven using oven mitts and let cool slightly.

# SPICY MUSSELS IN WHITE WINE

**Prep time: 10 minutes | Cook time: 10 minutes | serves 2**

2 tablespoons butter
3 large garlic cloves, minced
⅓ cup white wine
2 pounds (907 g) mussels or 30 littleneck
clams, scrubbed clean and rinsed well in a bowl
of cold water
1 tablespoon freshly squeezed lemon juice

2 tablespoons fresh parsley, minced
Freshly ground black pepper, to taste
TOOLS/EQUIPMENT
Cutting board
Knife
Large skillet with lid
Slotted spoon or tongs
Shallow serving dish

1. Cook the shellfish. In a large skillet over medium heat, melt the butter.
2. Add the garlic. When the garlic begins to sizzle, add the wine and shellfish. Increase the heat to high, cover, and steam, shaking the pan back and forth occasionally to allow even cooking until all mussels or clams have opened, about 5 minutes for mussels, and 6 minutes for clams. Discard any that do not open.
3. Season and serve. Using a slotted spoon or tongs, transfer the shellfish to a shallow serving dish, reserving the broth.
4. Add the lemon juice to the broth, then add the parsley and season with black pepper. Pour the broth over the shellfish and serve.
5. Add-Ins You can also add some crumbled cooked chorizo sausage to the hot broth with the shellfish.
6. Add a pinch or two of ground cayenne or red pepper flakes for a little spicy heat.

# MULTIGRAIN SPAGHETTI NOODLE SALAD

**Prep time: 10 minutes | Cook time: 25 minutes | serves 4**

Kosher salt, to taste
12 ounces (340 g) multigrain spaghetti
3 tablespoons red wine vinegar
2 tablespoons low-fat plain yogurt
2 teaspoons dijon mustard
2 scallions, thinly sliced
1 tablespoon chopped fresh dill (optional)
Freshly ground pepper, to taste
3 tablespoons extra-virgin olive oil
1 green bell pepper, thinly sliced
2 ounces sliced deli ham, cut into strips
2 ounces sliced cheddar cheese, cut into strips
½ small head romaine lettuce, thinly sliced

1.   Fill a large pot with water and season with salt. Bring to a boil over high heat.

2.   Add the spaghetti and cook as the label directs for al dente. Carefully drain the spaghetti in a colander set in the sink. Rinse the spaghetti in the colander under cold water until cool.

3.   Make the dressing: Combine the vinegar, yogurt, mustard, scallions, dill and ½ teaspoon salt in a large bowl and whisk until smooth; season with pepper. Drizzle in the olive oil, while whisking, until combined.

4.   Add the spaghetti, bell pepper, ham, cheese and lettuce to the dressing and toss to combine.

# CHEESE AND PARSLEY TOPPED PASTA

**Prep time: 10 minutes | Cook time: 20 minutes | serves 4**

⅓ cup olive or grape seed oil
5 large garlic cloves, sliced very thin
1 pound spaghetti or linguini
Kosher salt and freshly ground black pepper, to taste
1 cup freshly grated Parmesan cheese, divided
⅓ cup chopped fresh parsley, divided
TOOLS/EQUIPMENT
Cutting board
Knife
Grater
Large skillet
Wooden spoon
Large pot
Colander or strainer
Serving dish

1.   Cook the garlic. In a large skillet over low heat, heat the oil. Add the garlic and sauté until golden brown, 3 to 4 minutes. Remove from the heat and set aside.

2.   Cook the pasta. Using well salted water, cook the pasta according to package directions for al dente (firm). Once the pasta is done and ready to be drained, scoop out 1 cup of the cooking water and add it to the skillet with the garlic. Drain the pasta.

3.   Make the sauce. Heat the skillet with the water and garlic over medium-high heat, season with salt and pepper, stir to mix, and bring the mixture to a boil for 3 minutes.

4.   Mix the pasta and sauce. Meanwhile, return the pasta to the pot. Add the olive oil, season with salt and pepper, add about half the cheese and half the parsley, and toss well to combine. As soon as the sauce has been at a boil for 3 minutes, carefully pour the sauce into the pot with the pasta and toss. Let sit for 3 minutes for the flavors to mingle.

5.   Garnish and serve. Scrape the pasta into a serving dish, top with the remaining cheese and parsley, and serve.

# CHEESY RAVIOLI PASTA

**Prep time: 10 minutes | Cook time: 45 minutes | serves 6**

Nonstick cooking spray
2 cups pasta sauce
24 to 30 ounces frozen cheese
ravioli, divided
½ cup grated Parmesan cheese

1½ cups shredded mozzarella cheese
TOOLS/EQUIPMENT
Grater
8-by-8-inch baking dish
Aluminum foil

1. Preheat the oven. Preheat the oven to 375°F(191°C), and spray an 8-by-8-inch baking dish with cooking spray.

2. Layer and bake. Spread a layer of pasta sauce across the bottom of the baking dish, and cover the sauce with an even layer of ravioli.

3. Top with about half each of the remaining sauce, Parmesan cheese, and mozzarella.

4. Top the cheese with a second layer of ravioli, and top with the remaining sauce and cheeses.

5. Cover with foil and bake for 35 to 45 minutes, until the pasta is tender, removing the foil during the last 10 minutes of cooking.

6. Allow to rest for 10 to 15 minutes before serving.

# THYME HERBED CHICKEN SKILLET

**Prep time: 10 minutes | Cook time: 15 minutes | serves 4**

2 tablespoons apple cider
vinegar or white wine vinegar
2 tablespoons soy sauce
2 tablespoons pure maple syrup
8 boneless chicken thighs
Kosher salt and freshly ground
black pepper, to taste
2 tablespoons olive or grape
seed oil
Fresh thyme, for garnish

(optional)
TOOLS/EQUIPMENT
Small bowl
Whisk
Paper towel
Large nonstick skillet
Tongs
Spatula
Meat thermometer

1. Make the sauce. In a small bowl, whisk together the vinegar, soy sauce, and maple syrup. Set aside.

2. Prepare the chicken. Blot the chicken thighs dry with a paper towel, and season generously with salt and pepper.

3. Cook the chicken. In a large nonstick skillet over medium-high heat, heat the oil until shimmering. Using tongs, add the chicken thighs one at a time (the pan should sizzle as you add them). Cook for about 4 minutes on one side to brown the skin.

4. Turn them over and cook for an additional 4 minutes. Once both sides of the thighs are browned, pour in the sauce. When the sauce begins to bubble, reduce the heat to medium and continue cooking, flipping the thighs every minute or so.

5. Once the sauce has thickened, after about 5 minutes, check the thighs for doneness; a meat thermometer inserted into the thickest part of the thigh should read 165°F(74°C) when done (see Helpful Hint).

6. Garnish and serve. Sprinkle with fresh thyme, if desired, and serve.

# CHEESY MUFFIN TOPPED WITH BASIL

**Prep time: 10 minutes | Cook time: 10 minutes | serves 1**

¼ cup part-skim ricotta cheese
1 tablespoon pesto
Kosher salt and freshly ground
pepper, to taste

1 English muffin, split
2 tablespoons shredded Italian
cheese blend
Chopped fresh basil, for topping

1. Preheat the broiler. Mix together the ricotta and pesto in a small bowl. Season with salt and pepper.

2. Toast the English muffin in a toaster. Spread the ricotta mixture on the cut sides of the English muffin. Sprinkle with the shredded cheese.

3. Place the English muffin halves on a baking sheet, carefully place under the broiler and broil until the cheese is browned and bubbling, about 3 minutes. Top with basil.

# CHEESY PASTA CHICKEN MEATBALLS

Prep time: 10 minutes | Cook time: 20 minutes | serves 4

1 pound (454 g) ground chicken
1 garlic clove, minced, or 1 tablespoon garlic paste
½ cup bread crumbs
Salt and Freshly ground black pepper, to taste
1 large egg
2 tablespoons fresh basil, chopped, or 1 tablespoon dried basil
16 ounces (170 g) pasta sauce
1 cup fresh or shredded mozzarella cheese
TOOLS/EQUIPMENT
Cutting board
Knife
Rimmed baking sheet
Large bowl
Spatula
Plastic wrap
Medium casserole dish
Nonstick cooking spray or olive oil

1.   Preheat the oven. Preheat the oven to 375°F(191°C). Spray a baking sheet with cooking spray or lightly coat with olive oil.

2.   Mix the ingredients. In a large bowl, combine the chicken, garlic, bread crumbs, salt, pepper, egg, and basil. Mix with clean hands or a spatula until combined. Cover with plastic wrap and refrigerate for 30 minutes.

3.   Form the meatballs and bake. Using clean hands, form the chicken mixture into meatballs. Arrange the meatballs, not touching each nother, on the prepared baking sheet. Bake for 10 to 12 minutes, until they begin to brown.

4.   Assemble the dish and serve. Pour the pasta sauce into a medium casserole dish. Place the baked meatballs in the dish, turning to coat with sauce.

5.   Top each meatball with a slice of mozzarella or a mound of shredded cheese.

6.   Return to the oven and cook for an additional 7 to 10 minutes, or until the sauce is bubbly and the cheese is melted. Serve hot.

# CITRUSY BUTTER CHICKEN

Prep time: 10 minutes | Cook time: 10 minutes | serves 4

4 boneless chicken breasts
2 teaspoons lemon-pepper seasoning
⅓ cup all-purpose flour
3 tablespoons butter
2 lemons, 1 sliced thinly into rounds, and the other juiced
2 tablespoons chopped or snipped fresh parsley
Lemon zest, for serving (optional)
TOOLS/EQUIPMENT
Cutting board
Knife
Grater (optional)
Wax paper
Mallet, rolling pin, or heavy pan
Shallow bowl
Plate
Large skillet
Spatula
Meat thermometer

1.   Pound the chicken. Place the chicken breasts between two pieces of wax paper. Using a mallet, pound the chicken to about ½-inch thickness. Season on both sides with the lemon-pepper seasoning.

2.   Coat the chicken. Spread the flour in a shallow bowl, and, one by one, dredge the chicken breasts until evenly coated. Place the coated chicken on a plate.

3.   Cook the chicken. In a large skillet over medium-high heat, melt the butter.

4.   Add the chicken in batches, and cook for 3 to 6 minutes on each side (depending on size and thickness, until the internal temperature reaches 165°F(74°C) on a meat thermometer). After you flip the chicken, add the lemon juice, swirling the pan around gently to distribute.

5.   Garnish and serve. Remove the chicken from the pan, pour any remaining sauce over the chicken, garnish with the parsley, lemon slices, and a little bit of lemon zest if desired, and serve.

# RED PEPPER SPICED PASTA CHICKEN

### Prep time: 10 minutes | Cook time: 20 minutes | serves 4

4 (6-ounce/170 g) skinless, boneless chicken breasts
Salt and Freshly ground black pepper, to taste
Olive oil
2 cups pasta sauce
4 (½-inch-thick) slices fresh mozzarella cheese

4 large pieces jarred or fresh roasted red peppers
Chopped fresh parsley (optional)
TOOLS/EQUIPMENT
Large nonstick skillet
Tongs or spatula
Small pot
Meat thermometer

1. Preheat the oven. Preheat the oven to 375°F(191°C). Season the chicken.

2. Season the chicken breasts with salt and pepper, and set aside. Cook the chicken and heat the sauce.

3. Pour enough oil into a large nonstick skillet to just cover the bottom. Heat over medium-high heat until the oil is shimmering.

4. Cook the chicken, turning once, until the outside is browned and the chicken is cooked through, 4 to 6 minutes per side depending on size, or until the internal temperature reaches 165°F(74°C) on a meat

thermometer. Meanwhile, in a small pot over medium heat, heat the pasta sauce.

5. Assemble the dish. Once the chicken is done cooking, place a slice of mozzarella on each piece of chicken, followed by a slice of roasted red pepper.

6. Place the stacks in the skillet over medium-low heat for 3 to 5 minutes, until the cheese begins to melt.

7. Spoon warm pasta sauce onto individual plates, place a stack on top, add a little more sauce over top, garnish with a little chopped parsley, if desired, and

# DIJON MUSTARD CHICKEN BAKE

### Prep time: 10 minutes | Cook time: 35 minutes | serves 6

6 to 8 boneless chicken breasts
Salt and Freshly ground black pepper, to taste
1 (10-ounce/283 g) box frozen chopped spinach, thawed
1 (8-ounce/226 g block) cream cheese, room temperature
4 scallions, chopped
⅓ cup grainy Dijon mustard

TOOLS/EQUIPMENT
Cutting board
Chef's knife
Baking sheet or large baking dish
Medium bowl
Meat thermometer
Nonstick cooking spray

1. Preheat the oven. Preheat the oven to 350°F(177°C), and coat a baking sheet or baking dish with cooking spray.

2. Prepare the chicken. Trim any fat off of each chicken breast, and season with salt and pepper. Carefully slice a "pocket" into each breast by slicing on the diagonal through the breast, almost halving it but leaving one side and bottom and edge intact, like a flap. Set aside.

3. Mix the stuffing. In small handfuls, squeeze all the water from the spinach. In a medium bowl, combine the spinach, cream cheese, and scallions, and season

with additional salt and pepper. Mix well, using clean hands if necessary.

4. Stuff and bake. Stuff each breast with plenty of the mixture. Pack it in, press it down, and pull the flap over the top. Place on the baking sheet. Spread the mustard over top of each breast.

5. Bake for 25 to 30 minutes until the meat is firm and opaque, any juices run clear, and a meat thermometer inserted in the thickest part of the breast, registers 165°F(74°C). Cook time will vary based on the thickness of the chicken breasts.

# MUFFIN TOPPED WITH CHICKEN SALAD

### Prep time: 10 minutes | Cook time: 10 minutes | serves 1

1 tablespoon mayonnaise
1 tablespoon sour cream
1 tablespoon Buffalo hot sauce
½ cup shredded rotisserie chicken (skin removed)
Kosher salt

1 English muffin split
Unsalted butter, at room temperature, for spreading
Finely chopped celery and carrots, for topping

1. Mix together the mayonnaise, sour cream and hot sauce in a small bowl. Stir in the chicken and season with salt.

2. Toast the English muffin in a toaster.

3. Spread butter on the cut sides of the English muffin and top with the chicken salad and some celery and carrots.

# CITRUSY PORK BAKE

Prep time: 10 minutes | Cook time: 25 minutes | serves 6

½ cup grape seed or olive oil
¾ cup freshly squeezed orange juice, plus the
zest of 2 oranges, zested, then juiced (¾ cup)
¼ cup freshly squeezed lime juice
Large handful fresh cilantro (about ½ cup)
4 tablespoons garlic paste or 4 garlic cloves
1 tablespoon fresh oregano leaves
12 fresh mint leaves
Kosher salt and freshly ground black pepper, to
taste
3 pounds (1360 g) pork tenderloin (typically
2 pieces in a package, each weighing 1¼ to 1½
pounds)
TOOLS/EQUIPMENT
Micro plane or zester
Food processor or blender
Shallow baking dish
Grill
Knife

1.  Blend the marinade. In a food processor or blender, combine the oil, orange juice, lime juice, cilantro, garlic, oregano, and mint, and pulse until the leaves and garlic are minced and the marinade is liquid.

2.  Toss in the orange zest, and stir to combine.

3.  Marinate the pork. Season the pork with salt and pepper, place in a shallow baking dish, and pour the marinade over top.

4.  Cover and refrigerate for 2 to 24 hours, turning the pork occasionally to coat in the marinade.

5.  Cook the pork. Make sure the grill is clean and oiled. Preheat the grill to medium-high, and place the pork directly onto the grates.

6.  Discard the marinade. Once grill marks appear on the bottom and the meat releases itself, after 3 to 4 minutes, turn the meat a quarter turn. Continue to cook; turning occasionally, for 12 to 14 minutes more.

7.  Pork is done when the internal temperature at the thickest part of the tenderloins is 145°F(63°C). Remove from the grill, tent with foil, and let rest for 5 minutes. Slice and serve.

# STEAK TORTILLA WITH AVACADO DIP

Prep time: 15 minutes | Cook time: 10 minutes | serves 6

½ tablespoon salt
1 teaspoon chili powder
1 teaspoon onion powder
½ teaspoon freshly ground black pepper
1½ pounds (680 g) flank steak
2 to 3 carrots
1 small red cabbage
Lemon Vinaigrette
½ tablespoon grape seed or olive oil, plus more
if needed
½ recipe Avocado Dip or guacamole, plus more
for serving
Flour tortillas, for serving
Chips, for serving
TOOLS/EQUIPMENT
1 small bowl and 1 medium bowl
Grater
Large skillet or sauté pan
Meat thermometer
Tongs
Cutting board
Chef's knife

1.  Rub the steak. In a small bowl, combine the salt, chili powder, onion powder, and pepper, and mix until blended. Rub the seasoning mix onto both sides of the steak, and allow the steak to sit at room temperature for 20 minutes.

2.  Make the slaw. Using the larger side of a grater, shred the carrots by holding the carrot on an angle for longer shreds (you should have about 1½ cups).

3.  Place the shredded carrots in a medium bowl. Quarter a small head of red cabbage, remove the core from one of the quarters.

4.  Slice the quarter crosswise into thin strips and place in the bowl with the carrots (you should have about 1 cup).

5.  Toss with the Lemon Vinaigrette, and, using your hands, massage the dressing into the shredded vegetables a bit. Set aside and allow the flavors to mingle.

6.  Fry the steak. In a large skillet or sauté pan over medium-high heat, heat the oil. Once the oil begins to shimmer and a first wisp of smoke comes off of it, carefully place the steak in the pan.

7.  Cook the steak until a meat thermometer registers 145°F(63°C) for medium (see chart here), typically 4 to 5 minutes per side, turning once with tongs. Add additional oil if the pan looks dry, and reduce the heat if the meat is starting to burn.

8.  Rest and slice. Transfer the steak to a cutting board and allow to rest for 10 minutes. Using a chef's knife or serrated bread knife, slice the steak into thin slices, going against the grain (see Pro Tip).

9.  Serve and enjoy. Assemble the tacos by placing the meat, Avocado Dip, and the vegetable slaw onto tortillas.

10. Serve chips alongside with extra Avocado Dip.

# CITRUSY HONEYED SALMON SKILLET

**Prep time: 5 minutes | Cook time: 10 minutes | serves 4**

¼ cup honey
3 tablespoons low-sodium soy sauce
1 tablespoon freshly squeezed lime juice
2 garlic cloves, minced
4 skinless salmon fillets
Kosher salt and freshly ground black pepper, to taste
1 to 2 tablespoons olive oil
Chopped scallions, for garnish

(optional)
TOOLS/EQUIPMENT
Cutting board
Knife
Small bowl
Whisk
Large nonstick sauté pan or skillet
Metal spatula
Large fork
Serving plate

1. Make the sauce. In a small bowl, whisk together the honey, soy sauce, lime juice, and garlic. Set aside.

2. Cook the salmon. Season the salmon fillets generously with salt and pepper. In a large nonstick sauté pan or skillet over medium-high heat, heat the olive oil until hot.

3. Add the salmon and reduce the heat to medium. Cook for 3 to 4 minutes.

4. Gently flip the fillets and cook for about 2 minutes more, until seared. Reduce the heat to low, and pour the sauce mixture onto the fillets.

5. Continue to cook for 45 to 60 seconds, and gently flip the fillets to coat the other side in the sauce. Remove from the heat if necessary to allow the sauce to cool down (see Troubleshooting).

6. Remove from the heat when the salmon is cooked to your liking. It should flake easily with a fork. Cook time will vary based on the thickness of the salmon fillets.

7. Glaze and serve. Transfer the fillets to a serving plate, reserving the sauce in the pan. Simmer the remaining sauce for another 30 to 60 seconds and spoon over the fillets.

8. Garnish with scallions, if desired, and serve.

# ZUCCHINI BAKE WITH VEGGIE MIX

**Prep time: 15 minutes | Cook time: 30 minutes | serves 4**

2 large zucchini
Salt and Freshly ground black pepper, to taste
Homemade Breakfast Sausage or 1 (12-ounce/340 g) package breakfast sausage patties or links
⅓ cup chopped Vidalia (sweet) onion
1 cup chopped pepper (green, red, or poblano work well)

⅓ cup chopped grape tomatoes
2 cups shredded mozzarella cheese, divided
TOOLS/EQUIPMENT
Cutting board
Chef's knife
Grater
Teaspoon
Large, rimmed baking sheet
Large nonstick skillet

1. Preheat the oven. Preheat the oven to 375°F(191°C).

2. Prepare the zucchini. Halve the zucchini lengthwise, and using a teaspoon, scrape out half to three-quarters of the insides, scraping out all of the seeds. Place the zucchini, flat-side down, on a large, rimmed baking sheet.

3. Bake the zucchini. Bake for 15 minutes. Remove from the oven, flip the zucchini over, and season the insides with salt and pepper.

4. Cook the sausage. Meanwhile, cut each sausage piece into quarters. In a large nonstick skillet over medium-high heat, cook the sausage for 3 minutes, turning occasionally. Add 3 tablespoons of water and the onion and pepper to the pan.

5. Cook the veggies. Continue to simmer until the sausage is cooked through and the pepper and onion are soft, about 7 minutes.

6. Add the tomatoes, and cook for another minute. Remove from the heat, add ½ cup of cheese, and stir until incorporated.

7. Fill the zucchini. Fill the zucchini with the vegetable mixture, and top with the remaining 1½ cups of cheese. Bake for 3 minutes, or until the cheese is melted, cool slightly, and serve.

# CHAPTER 6: QUICK SNACKS

# THE BEST MAPLE OATS GRANOLA

**Prep time: 10 minutes | Cook time: 45 minutes | Makes 3 cups**

⅓ cup maple syrup
¼ cup coconut oil
¼ cup packed light brown sugar
½ teaspoon vanilla extract
¼ teaspoon ground cinnamon
¼ teaspoon kosher salt
2 cups old-fashioned rolled oats
⅔ cup chopped walnuts or other nuts, such as almonds and pecans
⅓ cup pumpkin seeds or other seeds, such as chia seeds or flaxseed

**BAKING EQUIPMENT**
Measuring cups and spoons
Sheet pan
Parchment paper
Large mixing bowl
Rubber spatula
Oven-safe gloves

1. Preheat your oven to 350°F(177°C). Line a sheet pan with parchment paper.
2. In a large mixing bowl, combine the maple syrup, coconut oil, brown sugar, vanilla, cinnamon, and salt. Mix well with a spatula. Don't worry about any coconut oil lumps. They will melt when you bake. (See this page for measuring and mixing ingredients.)
3. Add the oats, nuts, and seeds. Stir well so that every morsel in your granola is coated with the maple syrup mixture.
4. Pour the granola onto the prepared sheet pan. Make sure to scrape every last bit out of your bowl. Spread out the granola mixture evenly.
5. Put the sheet pan in the oven. Bake for 10 minutes. Using oven-safe gloves, remove the pan, stir the granola, and return it to the oven. Bake for 15 minutes, or until the granola is a beautiful golden brown color.
6. Remove the sheet pan from the oven. Let the granola cool for 30 to 45 minutes, or until completely cool. Use your hands to break up the granola if there are large chunks. This will make some clumps, which is my favorite part!
7. Once cooled, pour yourself a bowl with some milk, and enjoy! The rest can be stored in an airtight jar in a cool, dry place for up to 1 month.

TIP: Instead of maple syrup, you can use honey or agave nectar.

# DELICIOUS CHOCO CHIP COOKIES

**Prep time: 10 minutes | Cook time: 40 minutes | Makes 24 cups**

1 cup (2 sticks) unsalted butter, softened
1 cup packed dark brown sugar
1 cup granulated white sugar
1 ½ tablespoons heavy cream
2 eggs, at room temperature
½ teaspoon kosher salt
1 ½ teaspoons vanilla extract
3 cups all-purpose flour
¾ teaspoon baking soda
½ teaspoon baking powder

2 cups semisweet chocolate chips
**BAKING EQUIPMENT**
Measuring cups and spoons
Sheet pan
Parchment paper
Electric hand mixer
Mixing bowl
Ice-cream scoop
Oven-safe gloves
Offset spatula
Wire rack

1. Preheat your oven to 375°F(191°C). Line a sheet pan with parchment paper.
2. Using an electric hand mixer in a mixing bowl, cream together the butter, brown sugar, and granulated white sugar for 2 minutes on high speed (see Creaming Butter and Sugar on this page).
3. Add the cream, eggs, salt, and vanilla (see Cracking an Egg on this page). Mix until combined and glossy.
4. Add the flour, baking soda, and baking powder. Mix until there are no visible dry spots.
5. Reduce the mixer speed to low, and fold in the chocolate chips.
6. Using an ice-cream scoop, scoop about 12 dough balls onto the sheet pan. Give them some room because they will expand and flatten (see Spooning Cookie Dough on this page).
7. Put the sheet pan in the oven. Bake for 10 to 12 minutes, or until the edges of the cookies are golden brown and they look delicious.
8. Using oven-safe gloves, remove the sheet pan from the oven. Transfer the cookies using an offset spatula to a wire rack to cool for about 10 minutes.
9. Repeat with the remaining dough or keep it in an airtight container in the refrigerator for up to 3 days or in the freezer for up to 3 months.

TIP: Putting the dough in the refrigerator for at least 30 minutes before baking can help you have chewier, tastier cookies.

# GARLICKY CRACKERS WITH SOFT CHEESE

Prep time: 10 minutes | Cook time: 50 minutes | Makes 2 cups of crackers

1 cup all-purpose flour, plus more for rolling
the dough
1 teaspoon Italian seasoning
1 teaspoon kosher salt
½ teaspoon garlic powder
½ teaspoon dried minced garlic
¼ teaspoon baking powder
¾ cup ice water
2 tablespoons olive oil
BAKING EQUIPMENT
Measuring cups and spoons
Sheet pan
Parchment paper
Nonstick cooking spray
Mixing bowl
Wooden spoon
Rolling pin
Oven-safe gloves
2 metal or plastic spatulas
Wire rack

1. Preheat your oven to 400°F(204°C). Line a sheet pan with parchment paper, and then spray it with cooking spray.
2. In a mixing bowl, combine the flour, Italian seasoning, salt, garlic powder, dried minced garlic, and baking powder.
3. Stream in the water and olive oil. Using a wooden spoon, stir until a firm dough forms.
4. Lightly flour a clean work surface and rolling pin. Turn out the dough onto the surface, and roll out until it is ¼ to ½ inch thick . With your hands, transfer the whole sheet of rolled out dough to the prepared sheet pan. You may need to ask for help to move the dough.
5. Put the sheet pan in the oven. Bake for 25 minutes, or until the dough is light golden brown on top.
6. Using oven-safe gloves, remove the sheet pan from the oven. With two spatulas, transfer the baked dough to a wire rack. It will crisp as it cools.
7. Using the rolling pin, break the baked dough until you get some cool, jagged crackers!
8. You can serve crackers with soft cheese. Any leftovers can be stored in an airtight container at room temperature for up to a week.

# CHEESY GOLDEN BREADSTICKS

Prep time: 10 minutes | Cook time: 1 hour 25 minutes | Makes 10 bread sticks

1 cup all-urpose flour, plus more for
preparing the work surface
2 tablespoons shredded parmesan cheese
1 teaspoon kosher salt
½ teaspoon dried parsley flakes
¼ teaspoon cracked black pepper
¼ teaspoon granulated white sugar
1 tablespoon olive oil
1 tablespoon unsalted butter, softened
¼ cup ice-cold water
BAKING EQUIPMENT
Measuring cups and spoons
Sheet pan
Parchment paper
Nonstick cooking spray
Mixing bowl
Wooden spoon
Dish towel or plastic wrap
Rolling pin
Oven-safe gloves

1. Preheat your oven to 350°F(177°C). Line a sheet pan with parchment paper, then spray the parchment paper with cooking spray.
2. In a mixing bowl, add the flour, cheese, salt, parsley, pepper, and granulated white sugar. Stir until combined.
3. Add the oil and butter. Stir until combined.
4. Stream in the water slowly, stirring until it forms a shaggy dough.
5. Lightly flour a clean work surface. Turn the dough out onto the surface. Knead for 5 minutes, or until soft
6. Divide the dough into 10 equal balls. Let them rest for 10 minutes, covered loosely with a dish towel or plastic wrap.
7. Roll each dough ball out to about 10 inches long. (You want them long and thin to fit the length of your sheet pan. I like to use my hands to make them cylindrical.) Place on the prepared sheet pan.
8. Put the sheet pan in the oven. Bake for 35 to 40 minutes, or until the breadsticks are a beautiful golden brown color.
9. Using oven-safe gloves, remove the sheet pan from the oven. Let the breadsticks cool for 30 minutes.

# SCALLION SALMON WRAPS WITH CHEESE

**Prep time: 10 minutes | Cook time: 20 minutes | serves 4**

CRUST
1½ cups all-purpose flour, plus more for dusting
1 stick (4 ounces (113 g) unsalted butter, cubed and frozen
½ teaspoon kosher salt
1 large egg, beaten
2 tablespoons ice water, plus more if needed
"EVERYTHING BAGEL" SEASONING
2 tablespoons poppy seeds
2 tablespoons toasted sesame seeds
2 tablespoons dried garlic

2 tablespoons dried onion
4 teaspoons kosher salt
FILLING
6 ounces (170 g)scallion cream cheese, at room temperature
1 large egg
¼ teaspoon kosher salt
¼ teaspoon freshly ground black pepper
2 ounces smoked salmon, finely chopped (about ¼ cup)
2 large tomatoes (about 1½ pounds), thinly sliced
1 large egg

1. Make the crust: In a food processor, combine the flour, butter, and salt and pulse until the mixture is sandy, with a few pea-size pieces of butter still visible, about 1 minute.

2. Add the egg and ice water and pulse until moistened and the dough is starting to pull away from the sides of the bowl, about 30 seconds. (If the dough is still dry, add more ice water 1 teaspoon at a time; do not over process.)

3. Shape the dough into a 1-inch-thick disc and wrap it tightly with plastic wrap.

4. Transfer to the refrigerator to chill for at least 30 minutes or up to 3 days.

5. Make the "everything bagel" seasoning: In a small jar, combine the poppy seeds, sesame seeds, dried garlic, dried onion, and salt. Seal the jar and shake until well combined. (Store for up to 3 months.)

6. Position a rack in the center of the oven and preheat the oven to 400°F(204°C).

7. Make the filling: In a large bowl, using an electric mixer with the whisk attachment, beat the cream cheese and egg on medium-high speed until smooth, about 1 minute. Stir in the salt and pepper.

8. Pull off a 15-inch-long piece of parchment paper and dust it lightly with flour. Remove the chilled dough from the freezer, unwrap it, and place it on the parchment.

9. Using a rolling pin, roll the dough into a 12-inch-diameter round. Using the parchment as support, transfer the dough on the parchment to a baking sheet

10. Spoon the cream cheese mixture into the center of the dough and spread it into an even layer, leaving a 2-inch border around the edges. Scatter the smoked salmon over the cream cheese.

11. Arrange the tomatoes on top, overlapping the slices slightly so the cream cheese mixture is completely covered. Fold the bare edges of the dough up and over the tomatoes.

12. In a small bowl, whisk together the egg and 2 tablespoons water to make an egg wash. Brush the egg wash onto the crust and, while still moist, sprinkle the crust with the 1½ tablespoons of "everything bagel" seasoning. (Reserve the rest of the jar for another use.)

13. Bake until the crust is deeply golden brown and the tomatoes are soft, about 40 minutes. Let the tart rest on the baking sheet for 10 minutes, and then use the parchment to transfer it to a wire rack. Let cool to room temperature, about 20 minutes, before slicing and serving.

14. Wrap any leftovers in plastic wrap and store in the refrigerator for up to 2 days.

# CINNAMON SPICED PUMPKIN PIE

**Prep time: 10 minutes | Cook time:1 hour 30 minutes | serves 12**

1 refrigerated ready-to-use piecrust (for a 9-inch pie), softened as label directs
3 large eggs
¼ cup packed light brown sugar
1 (15-ounce) can pure pumpkin
½ cup whole milk

1 teaspoon vanilla extract
¾ teaspoon ground cinnamon
¾ teaspoon ground ginger
½ cup plus 6 tablespoons pure maple syrup
1 cup heavy cream
¼ teaspoon kosher salt

1. Heat oven to 350°F(177°C). Line 9-inch pie plate with piecrust. Gently press dough against bottom and up side of pie plate without stretching it. Tuck overhang under and crimp to form raised edge. Refrigerate until ready to fill.

2. In large bowl with wire whisk, beat eggs, brown sugar, pumpkin, milk, vanilla, cinnamon, ginger, ½ cup maple syrup, ¼ cup cream, and salt until combined.

3. Pour pumpkin mixture into prepared pie shell. Bake for 60 to 65 minutes or until edge of filling is just set but center still jiggles slightly and crust is golden brown. Cool pie on wire rack to room temperature.

4. About 10 minutes before serving, in large bowl with mixer on medium-high speed, beat remaining ¾ cup cream and remaining 6 tablespoons maple syrup until soft peaks form. Serve with pie.

# APPLE BAKE WITH STREUSEL TOPPING

**Prep time: 10 minutes | Cook time: 1 hour 15 minutes | Makes 9x3 inch dish**

For the streusel topping:
1 ½ cups (3 sticks) unsalted butter, melted, plus
more for greasing the baking dish
2 ½ cups rolled oats
1 cup packed light brown sugar
1 cup all-purpose flour
1 teaspoon vanilla extract
½ teaspoon kosher salt
½ teaspoon ground cinnamon
For the baked apple mix:
7 to 8 cups cored, peeled, diced apples, such as a Granny Smith and Gala about 5 large apples)
½ cup granulated white sugar
2 tablespoons water
1 ½ teaspoons cornstarch
1 teaspoon ground cinnamon
Juice of ½ lemon
BAKING EQUIPMENT
Knife
Measuring cups and spoons
9 x 13-inch baking pan
2 large mixing bowls
Wooden spoon
Oven-safe gloves

To make the streusel topping:

1. Preheat your oven to 375°F(191°C). Grease a 9 x 13-inch baking pan with butter.

2. In a large mixing bowl, using a wooden spoon, combine the melted butter, oats, brown sugar, flour, vanilla, salt, and cinnamon. Set aside.

3. To make the baked apple mix:

4. In another large mixing bowl, combine the apples, granulated white sugar, water, cornstarch, cinnamon, and lemon juice. Stir until fully combined and the apples are well coated.

5. Pour the apples into the prepared baking pan. Top with the streusel.

6. Put the baking pan in the oven. Bake for 35 to 40 minutes, or until bubbly and golden brown.

7. Using oven-safe gloves, remove the baking pan from the oven. Let cool for 20 minutes before serving.

# MOM'S SPECIAL IRISH BREAD

**Prep time: 10 minutes | Cook time: 1 hour 30 minutes | Makes 1 loaf**

4 cups all-purpose flour, plus
more for rolling
the dough
¼ cup granulated white sugar
½ teaspoon kosher salt
1 tablespoon baking powder
1 teaspoon baking soda
½ cup (1 stick) unsalted butter, softened
1 large egg
1 cup plus 1 tablespoon buttermilk
BAKING EQUIPMENT
Measuring cups and spoons
Sheet pan
Parchment paper
Mixing bowl
Rubber spatula
Knife
Pastry brush
Oven-safe gloves

1. Preheat your oven to 375°F(191°C). Line a sheet pan with parchment paper.

2. In a mixing bowl, use a spatula to stir together the flour, sugar, salt, baking powder, and baking soda.

3. Add the butter, egg, and 1 cup of buttermilk. Stir until a wet dough forms.

4. Lightly flour a clean work surface and your hands. Pour the dough out onto the surface, and knead for about 2 minutes, or until it is no longer wet and sticky.

5. Shape the dough into a dome about 8 inches across, and score it with a knife (see Shaping and Scoring Dough, below).

6. Brush the dough with the remaining 1 tablespoon of buttermilk. Transfer to the prepared sheet pan.

7. Put the sheet pan in the oven. Bake for 1 hour, or until a toothpick inserted into the center of the bread comes out clean.

8. Using oven-safe gloves, remove the sheet pan from the oven. Let the bread cool for 1 hour.

# YUMMY VANILLA FROSTED BUTTER CAKE

**Prep time: 10 minutes | Cook time: 1 hour 15 minutes | makes one 9 x 13-inch cake**

**For the cake:**
½ cup (1 stick) unsalted butter, softened, plus more for greasing the pan
1 ½ cups all-purpose flour
1 teaspoon baking powder
½ teaspoon baking soda
1 ¼ cups granulated white sugar
¼ cup packed light brown sugar
3 large eggs, at room temperature
½ cup buttermilk, at room temperature
½ cup grape seed oil
1 tablespoon vanilla extract
¾ teaspoon kosher salt
**For the frosting:**

4 ½ cups powdered sugar
1 cup (2 sticks) unsalted butter, softened
1 teaspoon vanilla extract
3 tablespoons whole milk
Sprinkles, for decorating (optional)
**BAKING EQUIPMENT**
Measuring cups and spoons
9 x 13-inch cake pan
Parchment paper
Sifter
3 mixing bowls
Electric hand mixer
Oven-safe gloves
Whisk attachment for mixer
Offset spatula

To make the cake:

1. Preheat your oven to 350°F(177°C). Line a 9 x 13-inch cake pan with parchment paper, and grease the parchment paper with butter

2. Sift together the flour, baking powder, and baking soda into a mixing bowl

3. Using an electric hand mixer in another mixing bowl, beat together the butter, granulated white sugar, and brown sugar on medium speed for 2 minutes

4. Add the eggs. Beat for about 4 minutes, or until the mixture is pale yellow, fluffy, and doubled in size.

5. Combine the buttermilk and oil in a measuring cup with a spout, and stream them into the batter while still beating. Add the vanilla and salt.

6. Add the flour mixture, and mix until there are no dry spots in the batter.

7. Turn off the mixer. Pour the batter into the prepared pan.

8. Put the cake pan in the oven. Bake for 20 to 25 minutes, or until a toothpick inserted into the center of the cake comes out clean and the edges are slightly browned.

9. Using oven-safe gloves, remove the cake pan from the oven, and let cool.

To make the frosting:

10. Sift the powdered sugar into a mixing bowl to remove any lumps.

11. Add the butter and vanilla. Using an electric hand mixer, whisk on medium speed until smooth and thick.

12. Whisk in the milk 1 tablespoon at a time until you get a smooth, soft texture.

13. Turn off the mixer. Using an offset spatula, ice the top of the cake until you reach the edges. (You will have a lot of frosting, so pile it on!) Decorate with sprinkles (if using).

# COCOA DUSTED MERINGUES

**Prep time: 10 minutes | Cook time: 1 hour 30 minutes | Makes 12 cookies**

3 large eggs, cold
½ teaspoon cream of tartar
1 cup granulated white sugar
1 teaspoon vanilla extract
¼ cup cocoa powder (optional)
**BAKING EQUIPMENT**
Measuring cups and spoons
Sheet pan

Parchment paper
Mixing bowl, plus 2 small bowls
for separating
the eggs
Electric hand mixer
Oven-safe gloves
Sifter or fine-mesh sieve

1. Preheat your oven to 225°F (107°C). Line a sheet pan with parchment paper.

2. Separate the egg whites from the yolks, placing the whites in a super clean mixing bowl (see Separating Eggs on this page).

3. Add the cream of tartar to the egg whites. Using an electric hand mixer, mix on low speed. Once you get some foam, raise the speed to medium. Once the mixture turns white, raise the speed to high (see Whipping Egg Whites on this page).

4. Add the sugar 1 tablespoon at a time so the egg whites can get big, fluffy, and glossy. If you see any sugar grains, keep mixing! You want your egg white mixture to be smooth.

5. Once the mixture is fluffy, add the vanilla. Continue whisking until fully mixed.

6. Turn off the mixer. Take 1 heaping tablespoon of your meringue, and spoon onto the prepared baking sheet. Repeat with the remaining meringue, leaving room in between (see Spooning Batter on this page).

7. Put the sheet pan in the oven. Bake for 1 hour. Don't peek!

8. Turn off the oven. Leave the sheet pan inside for 1 hour to completely dry the meringues. Keep the oven door closed as it could deflate and crack them.

9. Using oven-safe gloves, remove the sheet pan from the oven. Let cool for 45 minutes. Dust the meringues with the cocoa powder (if using)

# VANILLA FLAVORED BANANA WALNUT BREAD

**Prep time: 10 minutes | Cook time: 1 hour 20 minutes | Makes 1 loaf**

2 bananas, brown or freckled
2 large eggs, at room temperature
1 cup granulated white sugar
½ cup packed dark brown sugar
¾ cup grape seed oil
1 ½ teaspoons vanilla extract
½ teaspoon kosher salt
1 ¾ cups all-purpose flour
1 ½ teaspoons baking powder
¾ cup walnuts (optional)
BAKING EQUIPMENT
Measuring cups and spoons
9 x 5-inch metal loaf pan
Parchment paper
Nonstick cooking spray
Mixing bowl
Fork
Electric hand mixer
Rubber spatula
Oven-safe gloves
Knife

1.  Preheat your oven to 350°F(177°C). Line a 9 x 5-inch metal loaf pan with parchment paper, and then spray it with cooking spray.

2.  In a mixing bowl, mash the bananas with a fork.

3.  Add the eggs, granulated white sugar, brown sugar, oil, vanilla, and salt. Using an electric hand mixer, mix on medium speed for 3 to 5 minutes, or until smooth and creamy.

4.  Add the flour and baking powder. Mix to combine well.

5.  Using a spatula, fold in the walnuts (if using).

6.  Transfer the dough to the prepared loaf pan.

7.  Put the loaf pan in the oven. Bake for 1 hour to 1 hour and 5 minutes, or until a toothpick inserted into the center of the bread comes out clean.

8.  Using oven-safe gloves, remove the loaf pan from the oven. Let the bread cool for about 35 minutes.

9.  Remove the bread from the pan, and slice. Place leftover banana bread in an airtight container lined at the bottom with a paper towel. It can be stored at room temperature for up to 4 days.

# BLUEBERRY CRUMBLE WITH ICE-CREAM

**Prep time: 10 minutes | Cook time: 1 hour | Makes 9x3 inch crumble**

For the blueberries:
6 cups fresh blueberries
Juice of 1 lemon
2 tablespoons granulated white sugar
¼ cup all-purpose flour
1 tablespoon vanilla extract
For the crumble topping:
3 full-size Graham crackers
½ cup granulated white sugar
½ cup all-purpose flour
⅓ cup unsalted butter, softened
1 tablespoon packed light brown sugar
1 teaspoon vanilla extract
¼ teaspoon salt
BAKING EQUIPMENT
Measuring cups and spoons
Zip-top bag
Rolling pin
9 x 13-inch baking pan
Wooden spoon
Mixing bowl
Fork
Oven-safe gloves

To make the blueberries:

1.  Preheat your oven to 350°F(177°C). In a 9 x 13-inch baking pan combine the blueberries, lemon juice, granulated white sugar, flour, and vanilla. Stir well. Set aside.

2.  To make the crumble topping: Put the graham crackers in a zip-top bag, and seal it. Using a rolling pin, smash the crackers. They do not have to be super fine crumbs.

3.  In a mixing bowl, using a fork, mix together the granulated white sugar, flour, graham cracker crumbs, butter, brown sugar, vanilla, and salt until a crumbly mixture forms.

4.  Pour the crumble on top of the blueberry mixture. Put the baking pan in the oven. Bake for 35 minutes, until the center is bubbling.

5.  Using oven-safe gloves, remove the baking pan from the oven. Serve the crumble warm with ice-cream.

# CHOCO CAKE WITH GANACHE ICING

**Prep time: 10 minutes | Cook time: 1 hour 15 minutes | Makes 9x3 inch cake**

**For the chocolate cake:**
1 cup (2 sticks) unsalted butter, plus more for greasing the pan
1 cup water
⅓ cup cocoa powder
2 cups all-purpose flour
1 teaspoon baking powder
1 teaspoon baking soda
2 cups granulated white sugar
¼ teaspoons kosher salt
½ cup buttermilk
2 large eggs, at room temperature
1 teaspoon vanilla extract
**For the ganache icing:**
1 cup dark or semisweet chocolate chips
½ cup heavy cream

**BAKING EQUIPMENT**
Measuring cups and spoons
9 x 13-inch baking pan
Parchment paper
Saucepan
Wooden spoon
2 mixing bowls
Microwave-safe bowl
Rubber spatula
Oven-safe gloves
Knife
Whisk
Offset spatula

To make the chocolate cake:

1. Preheat your oven to 375°F(191°C). Line a 9 x 13-inch cake pan with parchment paper, and grease the parchment paper with butter.

2. In a saucepan, bring the butter and water to a boil over medium-high heat. Remove from the heat.

3. Add the cocoa powder, and stir until it is smooth. Set aside for about 10 minutes, or until cooled.

4. In a mixing bowl, combine the flour, baking powder, baking soda, sugar, and salt.

5. In a microwave-safe bowl, warm the buttermilk in the microwave for 10 seconds at a time, at 20 percent power, until it reaches room temperature (about 30 seconds total). Stir each time you remove the buttermilk from the microwave.

6. Add the buttermilk, eggs, and vanilla to the dry ingredients. Using a wooden spoon, stir to combine.

7. Add the cocoa powder and butter mixture. Stir until fully mixed.

8. Transfer the batter to the prepared baking pan.

9. Put the baking pan in the oven. Bake for 25 to 30 minutes, or until a toothpick inserted into the center of the cake comes out clean.

10. Using oven-safe gloves, remove the pan from the oven. Let the cake cool completely.

To make the ganache icing:

11. Put the chocolate chips in a mixing bowl and set aside.

12. In a microwave-safe bowl, warm the heavy cream in the microwave on 100 percent power for about 45 seconds, or until it starts to bubble. Make sure it doesn't boil or bubble over.

13. Pour the warm cream over the chocolate chips. Allow it to sit for about 3 to 4 minutes then gently stir the cream and chocolate with a whisk until smooth.

14. Using an offset spatula, ice the top of the cake until the ganache reaches the edges.

# HOMEMADE ALMOND COOKIES

**Prep time: 10 minutes | Cook time: 1 hour 10 minutes | makes 4 dozen cookies**

3¾ cups all-purpose flour
2 teaspoons baking powder
½ teaspoon salt
3 large eggs
1 cup sugar
¾ cup vegetable oil
2 teaspoons vanilla extract
¼ teaspoon almond extract
1 teaspoon freshly grated orange peel
1 cup slivered blanched almonds, toasted and coarsely chopped

1. Preheat oven to 350°F(177°C). In large bowl with wire whisk, mix flour, baking powder, and salt.

2. In large bowl with mixer on medium speed, beat eggs and sugar until light lemon-colored. Add oil, extracts, and orange peel, and beat until blended. With wooden spoon, beat in flour mixture until combined. Stir in almonds.

3. Divide dough in half. On large ungreased cookie sheet, drop each half of dough by spoonfuls down length of cookie sheet. With lightly floured hands, shape each half of dough into 12-inch-long log, 4 inches apart (dough will be slightly sticky).

4. Bake for 30 minutes or until dough is light-colored and firm. Cool logs on cookie sheet on wire rack for 10 minutes or until easy to handle. Arrange oven racks in top and bottom thirds of oven.

5. Transfer logs to cutting board. With serrated knife, cut each log crosswise into ½-inch-thick slices. Place slices, cut side down, on 2 ungreased cookie sheets.

6. Bake for 7 to 8 minutes or until golden, rotating cookie sheets between upper and lower racks halfway through baking. With metal spatula, transfer cookies to wire racks to cool completely.

# COCONUT CHOCO BITES

**Prep time: 10 minutes | Cook time: 25 minutes | serves 8**

1 cup shredded sweetened coconut
1 cup salted gluten-free pretzels, crushed into small pieces
½ cup rice flour
½ cup coconut oil, melted
3 tablespoons brown sugar
2 tablespoons unsweetened cocoa
1 cup coconut milk
6 ounces (170 g) dark chocolate, finely chopped
Pinch salt
Pomegranate seeds, for garnish, optional

1. Preheat oven to 375°F(191°C). Grease 9-inch tart pan with removable bottom.
2. In large bowl, combine shredded coconut, pretzels, rice flour, melted coconut oil, sugar, and cocoa. Transfer to prepared tart pan. With your hands, firmly press mixture into bottom and up side of pan in even layer; place on cookie sheet. Bake for 10 minutes. Cool crust completely on wire rack.
3. In small saucepan, heat coconut milk over medium heat until just bubbling at edges, whisking occasionally. Place chocolate and salt in medium heatproof bowl.
4. Pour hot coconut milk over chocolate. Let stand for 5 minutes. Gently whisk until smooth.
5. Pour into tart shell. Refrigerate, uncovered, for 2 hours or until set. Once set, tart can be made ahead, covered with plastic wrap, for up to 2 days. To serve, garnish with pomegranate seeds, if using.

# CINNAMON SPICED MINI MUFFINS

**Prep time: 10 minutes | Cook time: 45 minutes | Makes 36 mini muffins**

¾ cup applesauce
½ cup granulated white sugar
½ cup packed light brown sugar
1 large egg
1 ¼ cups all-purpose flour
½ teaspoon baking powder
1 teaspoon ground cinnamon
⅛ teaspoon ground nutmeg
2 cups peeled, cored, and diced apples, such as Granny Smith and Fuji (about 4 large apples)
BAKING EQUIPMENT
Knife
Cutting board
Measuring cups and spoons
Mixing bowl
Whisk
Rubber spatula
Silicone mini muffin mold
Oven-safe gloves

1. Preheat your oven to 350°F(177°C).
2. In a mixing bowl, whisk together the applesauce, granulated white sugar, brown sugar, and egg until combined and light yellow.
3. Add the flour, baking powder, cinnamon, and nutmeg. Whisk until you get a smooth batter.
4. Fold in the apples using a spatula.
5. Fill the cups in a silicone mini muffin mold three-quarters full with the batter.
6. Put the muffin mold in the oven. Bake for 15 minutes until golden brown on top.
7. Using oven-safe gloves, remove the muffin mold from the oven. Let the muffins cool for 30 minutes. Leftover muffins can be stored in an airtight container at room temperature for up to 2 days.
TIP: You can use a metal muffin tin, but be sure to grease the pan. Using a silicone mold allows your mini muffins to pop out cleanly for fast removal. However, a silicone mold is less firm, so ask an adult for help when placing it in the oven.

# GRANDMA'S BEST BLONDIES

**Prep time: 10 minutes | Cook time: 50 minutes | Makes 8 blondies**

1 cup all-purpose flour
½ teaspoon baking powder
¼ teaspoon baking soda
1 cup packed dark brown sugar
½ cup (1 stick) unsalted butter, at room temperature
1 ½ teaspoons vanilla extract
½ teaspoon kosher salt
2 large eggs, at room temperature
⅓ cup white chocolate chips
**BAKING EQUIPMENT**

Measuring cups and spoons
8 x 8-inch glass baking pan
Parchment paper
Nonstick cooking spray
Sifter
2 mixing bowls
Electric hand mixer
Rubber spatula
Oven-safe gloves
Knife

1. Preheat your oven to 350°F(177°C). Line an 8 x 8-inch glass baking pan with parchment paper, then spray the parchment paper with cooking spray.

2. Make sure you have some extra parchment hanging off all the sides to make it easy to take the blondies out of the pan later.

3. Sift the flour, baking powder, and baking soda into a mixing bowl.

4. Using an electric hand mixer in another mixing bowl, mix the brown sugar, butter, vanilla, and salt on high speed for about 2 minutes, or until combined.

5. Reduce the speed to low and add the eggs one at a time. Mix until fully combined.

6. Add the flour, baking powder, and baking soda, and mix until there aren't any dry bits.

7. Add the chocolate chips and gently mix them in.

8. Turn off the mixer. Pour the batter into the prepared baking pan. Using a spatula, smooth out the top of the batter. Tap the pan on the counter lightly a few times to get rid of any air bubbles.

9. Put the baking pan in the oven. Bake for 25 to 30 minutes, or until the edges and top are set and slightly browned.

10. Using oven-safe gloves, remove the baking pan from the oven. Let the Blondie cool, and then remove from the pan.

11. Cut into 8 pieces, and serve. Store leftover Blondie squares in an airtight container at room temperature for up to 2 days.

# HEALTHY PUMPKIN CHOCO BREAD

**Prep time: 10 minutes | Cook time: 60 minutes | Makes 1 loaf**

1 ½ cups all-purpose flour
½ teaspoon baking powder
½ teaspoon baking soda
1 teaspoon ground cinnamon
¼ teaspoon ground cloves
⅔ cup granulated white sugar
¼ cup packed dark brown sugar
⅓ cup grape seed oil
¾ teaspoon kosher salt
½ teaspoon vanilla extract
2 large eggs
1 ½ cups canned pumpkin purée
½ cup semisweet chocolate chips

**BAKING EQUIPMENT**
Measuring cups and spoons
Can opener
9 x 5-inch loaf pan
Parchment paper
Nonstick cooking spray
Sifter
2 mixing bowls
Whisk
Rubber spatula
Oven-safe gloves
Knife

1. Preheat your oven to 350°F(177°C). Line a 9 x 5-inch loaf pan with parchment paper, and then spray with cooking spray.

2. Sift the flour, baking powder, baking soda, cinnamon, and cloves into a mixing bowl.

3. Add the granulated white sugar, brown sugar, oil, salt, and vanilla. Whisk together.

4. Whisk in the eggs one at a time.

5. Add the pumpkin purée, and whisk until incorporated.

6. Using a spatula, fold in the chocolate chips.

Transfer the batter to the prepared loaf pan.

7. Put the loaf pan in the oven. Bake for 50 minutes, or until a toothpick inserted into the center of the loaf comes out clean.

8. Using oven-safe gloves, remove the loaf pan from the oven. Let the loaf cool for 1 hour, then slice and serve. Leftover pumpkin bread can be kept in an airtight container lined at the bottom with a paper towel. It can be stored at room temperature for up to 4 days.

# SUGAR COATED CINNAMON COOKIES

**Prep time: 10 minutes | Cook time: 45 minutes | Makes 20 cookies**

For the cinnamon-sugar coating:
¼ cup granulated white sugar
1 teaspoon ground cinnamon
¼ teaspoon kosher salt
For the cookies:
3 ⅓ cups all-purpose flour
2 teaspoons cream of tartar
1 teaspoon baking soda
1 teaspoon ground cinnamon
1 cup (2 sticks) unsalted butter, softened
1 cup granulated white sugar
1 teaspoon vanilla extract
½ teaspoon kosher salt
⅔ cup cookie butter
1 large egg, at room temperature
Baking equipment
Measuring cups and spoons
3 mixing bowls
Wooden spoon
Sheet pan
Parchment paper
Sifter
Electric hand mixer
Ice-cream scoop
Oven-safe gloves
Metal spatula
Wire rack

To make the cinnamon-sugar coating:
1.  In a mixing bowl, stir together the sugar, cinnamon, and salt. Set aside.
To make the cookies:
2.  Preheat your oven to 375°F(191°C). Line a sheet pan with parchment paper.
3.  Sift together the flour, cream of tartar, baking soda, and cinnamon into a mixing bowl.
4.  Using an electric hand mixer in another mixing bowl, cream together the butter, granulated white sugar, vanilla, and salt at high speed for 5 minutes, or until smooth and fluffy. Add the cookie butter and egg. Mix well.
5.  Add the flour mixture. Mix until there are no more dry flour bits left.
6.  Turn off the mixer. Using an ice-cream scoop, form the dough into balls, and roll in the cinnamon-sugar coating until fully coated. Place 10 balls on the prepared sheet pan. Give them some room because they will spread and flatten.
7.  Put the sheet pan in the oven. Bake for 10 to 12 minutes, or until the edges are lightly browned.
8.  Using oven-safe gloves, remove the baking sheets from the oven. Transfer the cookies to a wire rack to cool for 20 minutes.
9.  Repeat with the remaining dough or keep it in an airtight container in the refrigerator for up to 3 days or in the freezer for up to 3 months.

# SPICY CHEESY TWISTS

**Prep time: 10 minutes | Cook time: 20 minutes | makes about 44 twists**

1 cup finely grated Parmesan cheese (about 4 ounces (113 g)
1⅓ cups shredded sharp cheddar cheese (about 4 ounces (113 g)
4 tablespoons (½ stick) unsalted butter, at room temperature
1¾ cups all-purpose flour, plus more for rolling
1½ teaspoons kosher salt
½ teaspoon freshly ground black pepper
1 jalapeño pepper, halved, seeded, and minced
¼ cup plus 1 tablespoon heavy cream

1.  Line two baking sheets with parchment paper. In a food processor, combine the Parmesan, cheddar, butter, flour, salt, black pepper, and jalapeño and pulse in 5-second bursts until the mixture is sandy, with a few pea-size pieces of butter still visible, about 45 seconds.
2.  Drizzle in the cream and process until the dough forms a ball, about 15 seconds.
3.  On a lightly floured work surface, use a rolling pin to roll the dough into a 14-inch square about ⅛ inch thick. Halve the dough into two 7 × 14-inch rectangles, and then cut each rectangle crosswise into strips ½ inch wide. In the end you will have about 50 (7 × ½-inch) strips. Working with one at a time, gently twist each strip into a spiral.
4.  Transfer the strips to the prepared baking sheets, leaving ½ inch between them. Gently press the ends of the strips against the baking sheets so that the spirals hold their shape.
5.  Transfer the baking sheets to the refrigerator to chill the twists for at least 20 minutes or cover with plastic wrap and refrigerate for up to 3 days.
6.  Preheat the oven to 400°F(204°C).
7.  Bake until the twists are firm and golden, about 15 minutes. Let the twists rest on the baking sheets for 5 minutes, then transfer to a wire rack to cool completely. The twists will keep in an airtight container at room temperature for up to 1 week.

# CHEESY FRENCH TART

**Prep time: 10 minutes | Cook time: 20 minutes | serves 8**

1½ cups all-purpose flour
1 stick (4 ounces (113 g) unsalted butter, cubed and frozen
½ teaspoon kosher salt
5 large eggs
2 tablespoons ice water, plus more as needed
6 slices bacon, coarsely chopped
1 cup fresh or frozen corn kernels
Nonstick pan spray

1½ cups half-and-half
1 teaspoon kosher salt
½ teaspoon freshly ground black pepper
¼ teaspoon nutmeg, preferably freshly grated
3 scallions, thinly sliced
2 cups shredded sharp cheddar cheese

1. In a food processor, combine the flour, butter, and salt and pulse until the mixture is sandy, with a few pea-size pieces of butter still visible, about 1 minute.

2. Add 1 of the eggs and the ice water and pulse until the dough is moistened and starting to pull away from the sides of the bowl, about 30 seconds. (If the dough is still dry, add more ice water 1 teaspoon at a time; do not overprocess.)

3. Shape the dough into a 1-inch-thick disc and wrap it tightly with plastic wrap. Transfer to the refrigerator to chill for at least 30 minutes or up to 3 days.

4. In a medium skillet, cook the bacon over medium-high heat, stirring often, until crisp, about 8 minutes. Using a slotted spoon, transfer the bacon to a paper towel to drain.

5. Pour off and discard all but 1 tablespoon of the bacon drippings from the skillet. Add the corn to the skillet and cook over medium heat, stirring, until tender, 2 to 3 minutes. Set aside.

6. Preheat the oven to 400°F(204°C). Coat a 9½-inch deep-dish pie pan with pan spray.

7. Remove the chilled dough from the refrigerator and, using a rolling pin, roll it into a 12-inch round about ⅛ inch thick.

8. Gently transfer the dough to the prepared pie pan and trim and crimp the edges. Place the pan in the freezer to chill for 10 minutes.

9. Remove the pie pan from the freezer and line the crust with parchment paper. Fill with dried beans or pie weights.

10. Bake the crust until pale golden around the edges, about 20 minutes, then remove from the oven and carefully remove the parchment and the pie weights. Leave the oven on.

11. In a large bowl, whisk together the remaining 4 eggs, the half-and-half, salt, pepper, and nutmeg. Stir in the corn.

12. Sprinkle half the cheddar and the bacon over the bottom of the warm crust. Pour in the egg mixture and sprinkle with the remaining cheddar and bacon.

13. Bake until a toothpick inserted into the center of the quiche comes out clean, about 45 minutes. (If the crust looks too brown before the filling is set, wrap some foil around the edges or use a pie crust shield to protect it.) Let the quiche cool for 30 minutes before slicing and serving

# PEAS MATZO AND EGG SKILLET

**Prep time: 10 minutes | Cook time: 50 minutes | serves 6**

Nonstick cooking spray
1 tablespoon butter
1 bunch (about 1 pound) thin asparagus, trimmed and cut into 1-inch lengths
5 sheets matzo, broken into large chunks

5 large eggs
1 cup fresh basil leaves, chopped
1 cup frozen peas, thawed
1 tablespoon freshly grated lemon peel
1 teaspoon salt
½ teaspoon ground black pepper

1. Preheat oven to 350°F(177°C). Spray 8 x 8-inch baking dish with nonstick cooking spray.

2. In 12-inch skillet over medium heat, melt butter. Add asparagus and cook for 5 to 8 minutes or until crisp-tender. Remove skillet from heat and cool.

3. Meanwhile, in medium bowl, pour 1 cup warm water over matzo. Let stand for 5 minutes or until softened. Drain.

4. In large bowl with wire whisk, beat eggs. Stir in asparagus, matzo, basil, peas, lemon peel, salt, and pepper.

5. Pour into prepared baking dish. Bake for 40 minutes or until top is golden brown and center is set. Cooled frittata may be made ahead, covered with plastic wrap, and refrigerated for up to 3 days.

# HOMEMADE BUTTER COOKIES

**Prep time: 10 minutes | Cook time: 35 minutes | Makes 20 cookies**

¾ cup (1 ½ sticks) unsalted butter, softened
¾ cup granulated white sugar
1 large egg, at room temperature
1 teaspoon vanilla extract
¼ teaspoon kosher salt
2 cups all-purpose flour
½ teaspoon baking powder
½ teaspoon baking soda
BAKING EQUIPMENT:
Measuring cups and spoons
Sheet pan
Parchment paper
Electric hand mixer
Mixing bowl
Rubber spatula
Plastic wrap
Knife
Oven-safe gloves
Metal spatula
Wire rack

1.   Preheat your oven to 325°F(163°C). Line a sheet pan with parchment paper.
2.   Using an electric hand mixer on medium-high speed in a mixing bowl, cream the butter and granulated white sugar together for about 5 minutes, or until fluffy .
3.   Add the egg, vanilla, and salt. Mix for 1 minute. Add the flour, baking powder, and baking soda. Mix until fully combined.
4.   Turn off the mixer. Using a spatula, turn out the cookie dough onto a large sheet of plastic wrap. Wrap the dough, forming it into a log. Refrigerate for 1 to 2 hours, or until firm.
5.   Remove the dough log from the refrigerator and remove the plastic wrap. Cut the dough into about 20 equal slices, and place 10 on the prepared sheet pan. Refrigerate the rest.
6.   Put the sheet pan in the oven. Bake for 10 to 12 minutes, or until the cookies are very lightly browned on the edges and the bottoms.
7.   Using oven-safe gloves, remove the sheet pan from the oven. Transfer the cookies to a wire rack to cool.
8.   Repeat for remaining cookie slices or keep them in an airtight container in the refrigerator for up to 3 days or in the freezer for up to 3 months.

# HOMEMADE CORN BREAD AND HONEYED BUTTER

**Prep time: 10 minutes | Cook time: 55 minutes | Makes 1 9 inch loaf**

For the cornbread:
¼ cup (½ stick) unsalted butter, melted, plus more for greasing the pan
1 cup all-purpose flour
1 cup cornmeal
¼ cup granulated white sugar
1 teaspoon baking powder
¼ teaspoon baking soda
½ teaspoon kosher salt
1 cup milk
1 large egg
¼ cup grape seed oil
For the honey butter:
½ cup (1 stick) unsalted butter, softened
¼ cup honey
BAKING EQUIPMENT
Measuring cups and spoons
9-inch cake pan
Parchment paper
2 mixing bowls
Whisk
Oven-safe gloves
Wooden spoon

To make the cornbread:
1.   Preheat your oven to 400°F(204°C). Line a 9-inch cake pan with parchment paper, and grease the paper with butter.
2.   In a mixing bowl, combine the flour, cornmeal, granulated white sugar, baking powder, baking soda, and salt. Whisk well.
3.   Add the milk, egg, melted butter, and oil. Whisk until there are no dry bits and no lumps left. Pour the batter into the prepared cake pan.
4.   Put the cake pan in the oven. Bake for 22 minutes, or until a toothpick inserted into the center of the bread comes out dry.
5.   Using oven-safe gloves, remove the pan from the oven. Let the cornbread cool for 15 minutes.
6.   To make the honey butter: While the cornbread is cooling, in another mixing bowl, stir together the softened butter and honey until fully incorporated.
7.   Serve the cornbread warm with the honey butter. Cooled cornbread can be tightly wrapped in plastic wrap, and stored at room temperature for up to 3 days.

# THE BEST FUDGY COCOA BROWNIES

**Prep time: 10 minutes | Cook time: 50 minutes | Makes 8 brownies**

¾ cup all-purpose flour
¼ cup Dutch-processed cocoa powder
1 cup semisweet chocolate chips
⅓ cup unsalted butter
¾ cup granulated white sugar
1 tablespoon packed dark brown sugar
1 teaspoon vanilla extract
½ teaspoon kosher salt
2 large eggs, at room temperature
1 large egg yolk, at room temperature

**BAKING EQUIPMENT**
Measuring cups and spoons
8 x 8-inch glass baking pan
Parchment paper
Nonstick cooking spray
Sifter
2 mixing bowls
Microwave-safe bowls
Rubber spatula
Electric hand mixer
Oven-safe gloves
Knife

1. Preheat your oven to 325°F(163°C). Line an 8 x 8-inch glass baking pan with parchment paper, then spray the parchment paper with cooking spray. Make sure you have some extra parchment paper hanging off all the sides to make it easy to take the brownies out of the pan later.

2. Sift the flour and cocoa powder into a mixing bowl

3. In a microwave-safe bowl, melt ½ cup of chocolate chips. In another microwave-safe bowl, melt the butter. Combine both bowls and mix until smooth and silky.

4. In another mixing bowl, combine the granulated white sugar, brown sugar, vanilla, salt, eggs, and yolk. Using an electric hand mixer, mix on medium speed for 1 minute.

5. Add the butter and chocolate mixture to the egg mixture. Mix until fully combined.

6. Reduce the mixer speed to low. Add the flour mixture. Mix until there are no dry flour bits.

7. Slowly mix in the remaining ½ cup of chocolate chips.

8. Transfer the batter to the prepared baking pan. Tap the pan on the counter lightly a few times to get rid of any air bubbles. Put the baking pan in the oven.

9. Bake for 25 to 30 minutes or until the top is crackly and the sides are fully baked.

10. Using oven-safe gloves, remove the baking pan from the oven. Let the brownies cool, and then remove from the pan. Cut into 8 pieces, and serve.

TIP: You can store brownie squares in an airtight container at room temperature for up to 2 days.

# VANILLA CHOCO COOKIES

**Prep time: 10 minutes | Cook time: 60 minutes | Makes 20 cookies**

2 cups all-purpose flour
½ cup cocoa powder
1 teaspoon baking powder
1 cup (2 sticks) unsalted butter, softened
1 ¾ cups powdered sugar
¼ cup granulated white sugar
½ cup packed dark brown sugar
1 teaspoon vanilla extract
¼ teaspoon kosher salt
2 large eggs
2 cups chocolate chips, such as

a combination milk chocolate and semisweet
**BAKING EQUIPMENT**
Measuring cups and spoons
Sheet pan
Parchment paper
2 mixing bowls
Electric hand mixer
Ice-cream scoop
Oven-safe gloves
Metal spatula
Wire rack

1. Preheat your oven to 375°F(191°C). Line a sheet pan with parchment paper. Sift together the flour, cocoa powder, and baking soda into a mixing bowl.

2. In another mixing bowl, combine the butter, powdered sugar, granulated white sugar, brown sugar, vanilla, and salt. Using an electric hand mixer, mix on high speed for 3 minutes, or until pale yellow in color.

3. Add the eggs one at a time, and mix until fully incorporated.

4. Add the flour mixture. Mix until there are no dry bits.

5. Reduce the mixer speed to low. Slowly mix in the chocolate chips.

6. Turn off the mixer. Using an ice-cream scoop, scoop 10 dough balls out and place them onto the prepared sheet pan. Make sure to leave space between them because they will spread a bit.

7. Put the sheet pan in the oven. Bake for 12 minutes.

8. Using oven-safe gloves, remove the sheet pan from the oven. Using a metal spatula, transfer the cookies to a wire rack to cool for 15 minutes.

9. Repeat with the remaining dough or keep the remaining dough in an airtight container in the refrigerator for up to 3 days or in the freezer for up to 3 months.

# PRETZEL STEMS TOPPED PUMPKIN CAKE

**Prep time: 10 minutes | Cook time: 1 hour | makes 6**

Nonstick cooking spray
1 (15.25-ounce/ 432 g) box
yellow or chocolate cake mix
Orange and green gel food
coloring
2 cups confectioners' sugar
Orange and green crystal sugar
or candy decorations
Pretzel rods or sticks
Marzipan, for leaves

1. Preheat oven to 350°F(177°C). Spray 12 mini Bundt pans with nonstick cooking spray.
2. Prepare cake mix (tint with food coloring, if desired) and bake as directed, filling pans halfway with batter.
3. When cakes are done, unmold them onto wire rack and cool completely.
4. In 4-cup measuring cup, mix confectioners' sugar and 3 to 4 tablespoons water to make thick glaze. With sharp knife, trim bottom of each cake flat; assemble into pairs. Using a small amount of glaze drizzled on flat sides of cakes, attach pairs to form 6 pumpkins.
5. Drizzle pumpkin cakes with glaze and/or sprinkle with crystal sugar or candy decorations. Break pretzel rods to fit as stems. Moisten pretzels with water and roll in crystal sugar. Insert into centers of pumpkins.
6. Tint marzipan with green food coloring for leaves. Roll and cut as desired and place around pretzel stems. Let cakes stand until glaze is set.

# YUMMY CARAMELIZED NUT PIE

**Prep time: 10 minutes | Cook time: 1 hour | serves 12**

1 refrigerated ready-to-use piecrust (for a
9-inch pie), softened as label
directs
4 cups mixed unsalted pecans,
walnuts, and hazelnuts, toasted
1½ cups sugar
3 tablespoons light corn syrup
6 tablespoons unsalted butter,
cut into small pieces
½ teaspoon kosher salt
1 cup heavy cream
Flaked sea salt, optional

Line 9-inch pie plate with piecrust. Gently press dough against bottom and up side of plate without stretching it. Tuck overhang under and crimp to form raised edge.
2. Line crust with nonstick foil; fill with pie weights or dried beans. Bake for 15 minutes. Remove parchment and weights.
3. Bake for 5 to 10 minutes longer or until pastry just starts to turn golden. Transfer crust to wire rack; spread nuts in crust.
4. Reduce oven temperature to 350°F(177°C). In heavy-bottomed medium saucepan, place sugar, ½ cup water, and corn syrup. Without stirring, cook over medium-high heat for about 1 minute or until bubbles begin to form at edges, swirling pan occasionally.
5. Bring to a simmer, then increase heat to high and boil for 6 to 10 minutes or until mixture is a rich caramel color, swirling pan occasionally. Immediately remove pan from heat, add butter and kosher salt, and swirl pan until butter melts.
6. Return pan to medium heat, add cream (it will bubble up), and whisk for about 1 minute or until smooth, slightly thickened, and a deep amber color. Pour caramel over nuts; place pie in oven. Bake for 10 to 15 minutes or until filling is gently bubbling.
7. Cool pie completely on wire rack. Sprinkle with flaked sea salt, if using.

# YUMMY KNOTS WITH MARINARA SAUCE

**Prep time: 10 minutes | Cook time: 20 minutes | makes 12 garlic knots**

GARLIC BUTTER
8 tablespoons (1 stick/4 ounces (113 g) unsalted butter, divided
8 large garlic cloves, minced
DOUGH
2 cups all-purpose flour, plus more for shaping
1½ teaspoons instant (Rapid Rise) yeast
1 teaspoon garlic powder
1 tablespoon extra-virgin olive

oil, plus more for the bowl
FOR SERVING
2 tablespoons minced fresh flat-leaf parsley
2 tablespoons finely grated Parmesan cheese, plus more as needed
½ teaspoon kosher salt
Extra-virgin olive oil, as needed
1 cup marinara sauce, warmed

1. Make the garlic butter: In a small saucepan, melt 2 tablespoons of the butter over medium heat.

2. Stir in the garlic; reduce the heat to low, and cook, stirring often, until the garlic is soft and fragrant but not browned, about 3 minutes.

3. Add the remaining 6 tablespoons butter and swirl the pan until the butter has melted, about 1 minute. Strain the garlic butter through a fine-mesh sieve into a large bowl. Reserve the garlic solids in a small bowl. Set both bowls aside.

4. Make the dough: In the bowl of a stand mixer, whisk together the flour, yeast, and garlic powder. In a small bowl, whisk together the oil, reserved garlic solids, and ¾ cup warm water.

5. Attach the dough hook to the stand mixer and, with the mixer on medium-low speed, drizzle the oil-garlic mixture into the flour mixture and knead, scraping down the sides of the bowl as needed, until a sticky dough starts to come together, about 3 minutes. Increase the speed to medium-high and knead until the dough is smooth and shiny and pulling away from the side of the bowl, about 6 minutes more.

6. Transfer the dough to a lightly floured work surface and knead it once or twice. Turn the dough over, push, and shape it into a ball. Lightly grease a large bowl with oil, then place the dough in the bowl, seam-side down.

7. Cover the bowl with plastic wrap and transfer it to a warm spot to rest until the dough is doubled in size, about 1½ hours.

8. Transfer the dough to a lightly floured work surface. Using your hands, lightly stretch it into a 7 × 12-inch rectangle. With a long side facing you, use a sharp knife or a pizza cutter to cut the dough crosswise into 12 (1-inch-wide) strips. Cover the strips lightly with plastic wrap.

9. Line a baking sheet with parchment paper. Working with one at a time, place a dough strip on a lightly floured work surface and roll it into a 12-inch rope. Tie the rope into a loose overhand knot, tucking the ends underneath.

10. Transfer the knot to the prepared baking sheet and repeat with the remaining dough, leaving 2 inches of space between the knots. Lightly cover the baking sheet with plastic wrap or a kitchen towel and transfer it to a warm spot to rest until the knots have nearly doubled in size, about 1½ hours.

11. Preheat the oven to 475°F(246°C).

12. Measure out 2 tablespoons of the reserved garlic butter and brush it over the knots. Bake until deeply golden, about 12 minutes.

13. Meanwhile, whisk the parsley, Parmesan, and salt into the garlic butter remaining in the large bowl to combine,

14. While the knots are still warm, add them to the bowl with the garlic butter mixture and toss them until well coated (if the mixture looks a little dry, drizzle in a bit of oil). Serve immediately, with the marinara sauce on the side for dipping.

# SWEET BUTTER LOAF

**Prep time: 10 minutes | Cook time: 1 hour 15 minutes | serves 12**

4 cups all-purpose flour
¼ cup sugar
1 tablespoon baking powder
1½ teaspoons salt
1 teaspoon baking soda

6 tablespoons butter
1 cup dried currants
2 teaspoons caraway seeds
1½ cups low-fat buttermilk

1. Preheat oven to 350°F(177°C). Grease large cookie sheet.

2. In large bowl with wire whisk, mix flour, sugar, baking powder, salt, and baking soda. With pastry blender or 2 knives used scissors-fashion, cut in butter until mixture resembles coarse crumbs. Stir in currants and caraway seeds, then buttermilk, until flour is moistened.

3. Turn dough onto well-floured surface; knead dough 8 to 10 times, just until combined. Shape into flattened ball; transfer to prepared cookie sheet. Cut ¼-inch-deep X into top using a knife.

4. Bake 1 hour or until toothpick inserted in center of loaf comes out clean. Cool loaf completely on wire rack.

# SWEET VANILLA COOKIES

**Prep time: 10 minutes | Cook time: 1 hour 10 minutes | makes 3 dozen cookies**

3 cups all-purpose flour
¾ teaspoon baking powder
½ teaspoon salt
1 cup (2 sticks) butter, softened
1 cup sugar
1 large egg
2 teaspoons vanilla extract
1 teaspoon almond extract

1. Preheat oven to 375°F(191°C). In large bowl with wire whisk, mix flour, baking powder, and salt. In another large bowl with mixer on medium-high speed, beat butter and sugar until smooth.

2. Beat in egg, then extracts, occasionally scraping bowl with rubber spatula. Reduce speed to low; gradually beat in flour mixture just until blended.

3. Divide dough into 4 equal pieces; flatten each into a disk.

4. Wrap each disk tightly in plastic wrap and refrigerate for 30 minutes or until dough is firm but not hard.

5. For cutouts: Remove 1 disk of dough from refrigerator. On one half of lightly floured large sheet parchment paper, with floured rolling pin, roll dough ⅛ inch thick.

6. With floured cookie cutter, cut out shapes. With paring knife or small metal spatula, remove dough between cutouts. On other half of parchment, reroll the scraps of dough and cut out more shapes.

7. Slide parchment onto large cookie sheet. Bake for 10 to 12 minutes or until edges are golden. With spatula, transfer cookies to wire racks to cool completely. Repeat with remaining dough.

# CAYENNE PEPPER SPICED CEREAL MIX

**Prep time: 10 minutes | Cook time: 20 minutes | makes 12 cups**

3½ cups corn squares cereal (such as Corn Chex)
3½ cups wheat squares cereal (such as Wheat Chex)
2 cups pretzel fish (such as Goldfish) or other bite-size pretzels
1 cup oyster crackers
1 cup unsalted dry-roasted peanuts
1 stick (4 ounces (113 g) unsalted butter, melted
⅓ cup Worcestershire sauce
1 tablespoon plus 2 teaspoons Old Bay seasoning
½ teaspoon garlic powder
⅛ teaspoon cayenne pepper

1. Preheat the oven to 300°F. Line a baking sheet with parchment paper.

2. In a large bowl, combine the cereals, pretzels, oyster crackers, and peanuts. In a 4-cup measuring cup, stir together the melted butter, Worcestershire sauce, Old Bay seasoning, garlic powder, and cayenne.

3. Pour the butter mixture over the cereal mixture and stir gently with a rubber spatula until well combined.

4. Spoon the mixture onto the prepared baking sheet and spread it out into an even layer.

5. Bake until the mixture looks lightly toasted and smells fragrant, about 1 hour, tossing the mixture every 15 minutes. Let the mix cool on the baking sheets, then transfer to an airtight container and store for up to 2 weeks.

# GOLDEN PINWHEELS WITH CHEESE

**Prep time: 10 minutes | Cook time: 20 minutes | makes 24 pinwheels**

10 ounces frozen chopped spinach, thawed and drained
8 ounces (227 g) crumbled feta cheese, at room temperature
¼ cup sour cream
2 tablespoons chopped fresh dill
2 teaspoons crushed red pepper flakes

½ teaspoon garlic powder
½ teaspoon kosher salt
2 tablespoons all-purpose flour
2 sheets frozen puff pastry, thawed (from one 16-ounce /454 g package)
1 large egg, beaten

1. Sandwich the spinach between two layers of paper towels and press out any excess water.
2. In a medium bowl, combine the spinach, feta, sour cream, dill, red pepper flakes, garlic powder, and salt and mix to combine.
3. Dust a work surface with the flour and place the thawed puff pastry sheets on it. Divide the feta mixture in half and spoon it evenly over each pastry sheet, leaving a ½-inch border on all sides.
4. Starting with a long side, roll each puff pastry sheet into a log. Wrap the logs tightly with plastic wrap and set them seam-side down on a baking sheet. Freeze until firm, about 30 minutes. (To store longer, transfer the logs to an airtight freezer bag and freeze; they will keep for up to 2 months.)
5. Preheat the oven to 400°F(204°C). Line two baking sheets with parchment paper.
6. Remove the pastry logs from the freezer, unwrap, and place them seam-side down on your work surface. Slice each log crosswise into twelve ¾-inch-thick rounds.
7. Arrange the slices cut-side down on the prepared baking sheets. In a small bowl, mix the beaten egg with 1 tablespoon water to make an egg wash and brush it over the top and sides of each slice.
8. Bake until the pinwheels are puffed and golden brown, 15 to 20 minutes. Serve warm or at room temperature.

# PRETZELS WITH MELTED BUTTER

**Prep time: 10 minutes | Cook time: 20 minutes | makes 6 pretzels**

2¼ teaspoons instant (Rapid Rise) yeast
2 tablespoons honey
2 tablespoons unsalted butter, melted, plus more for serving
1 teaspoon kosher salt

2¾ cups all-purpose flour, plus more for dusting and shaping
1 tablespoon canola oil, for the bowl
3 tablespoons baking soda
1 large egg, beaten
Coarse kosher salt, for sprinkling

1. In a stand mixer fitted with the dough hook, whisk together 1 cup warm water, the yeast, honey, melted butter, and salt. Add the flour and knead on low speed until a smooth, elastic ball of dough forms, about 6 minutes.
2. Place the dough in a lightly oiled large bowl and turn to coat the dough with oil. Cover the bowl with plastic wrap or a kitchen towel and set aside in a warm place to rise until the dough has doubled in size, 45 minutes to 1 hour.
3. Punch down the dough, cover the bowl, and let rise until nearly doubled again, 30 to 40 minutes more.
4. Line two large baking sheets with parchment paper and dust the parchment lightly with flour.
5. Divide the dough into 6 equal pieces. Starting at the center and rolling outward, use the palms of your hands to roll each piece into a 20-inch-long rope (flour your hands if the dough is sticky).
6. Form the rope into a "U" shape, twist the ends of the rope around each other, then flip the twisted section down and press the ends lightly onto the bottom of the "U." Transfer the pretzel to the prepared baking sheets and repeat with the remaining dough pieces.
7. Position racks in the upper and lower thirds of the oven and preheat the oven to 450°F(232°C). At the same time, in a wide saucepan or large Dutch oven, bring 6 cups water and the baking soda to a boil.
8. Working in batches, use a spatula to carefully lower 2 pretzels into the boiling water. Cook the dough for 30 seconds, then use a spatula or tongs to flip the pretzels over and cook for 30 seconds more.
9. Use a slotted spoon to remove the pretzels from the water, letting any excess water drip off, and return them to the baking sheets. Repeat with the remaining pretzels in batches of 2.
10. Brush the pretzels with the beaten egg and sprinkle with coarse salt. Bake until the pretzels are deeply golden brown and shiny, 12 to 14 minutes, switching the pans from the top to bottom rack halfway through.
11. Brush the pretzels with melted butter and serve warm. Store leftovers at room temperature for up to 2 days or freeze in zip-top freezer bags for up to 1 month.

# CINNAMON SPICED BREAD PUDDING

Prep time: 10 minutes | Cook time: 1 hour 15 minutes | Makes one 9 inch cake pan

1 tablespoon unsalted butter, plus more for greasing the pan
½ cup raisins
1 cup milk
1 cup heavy cream
⅔ cup granulated white sugar
4 large eggs
1 ½ teaspoons vanilla extract
1 teaspoon ground cinnamon
6 cups torn day-old bread, such as a country loaf
BAKING EQUIPMENT
Measuring cups and spoons
9-inch cake pan
Parchment paper
Small bowl
Colander
Mixing bowl
Whisk
Oven-safe gloves

1.  Preheat your oven to 350°F(177°C). Line a 9-inch cake pan with parchment paper, and grease the parchment paper well with butter.

2.  In a small bowl of warm water, steep the raisins for 5 minutes, or until nice and plump. Drain well in a colander.

3.  In a mixing bowl, whisk together the milk, cream, sugar, butter, and eggs until a well-blended custard forms.

4.  Add the vanilla and cinnamon and whisk to combine. Put the bread in the prepared cake pan. Sprinkle the raisins over the bread. Drizzle the custard on top.

5.  Put the cake pan in the oven. Bake for 45 minutes, or until the bread is golden brown and crispy on top.

6.  Using oven-safe gloves, remove the pan from the oven. Let the bread pudding cool for 15 minutes. Serve warm with ice cream, if desired.

# OATS LOAF WITH SEEDS

Prep time: 10 minutes | Cook time: 20 minutes | makes one 8½ × 4½ inch loaf

Butter or nonstick pan spray
4 cups rolled oats
¼ cup chia seeds
2½ cups buttermilk
2 tablespoons extra-virgin olive oil
1½ tablespoons molasses
2 teaspoons baking soda
1 teaspoon kosher salt
⅓ cup plus 1 teaspoon flaxseeds
⅓ cup plus 1 tablespoon sunflower seeds

1.  Preheat the oven to 400°F(204°C). Coat an 8½ × 4½-inch loaf pan with pan spray and line it with parchment paper, leaving a few inches of overhang on both of the long sides. (This will help you lift the loaf out of the pan after baking.)

2.  In a large bowl, stir together the oats, chia seeds, and buttermilk until well combined. Set aside to allow the oats to soften and absorb the buttermilk, about 30 minutes.

3.  Stir in the oil, molasses, baking soda, salt, ⅓ cup of the flaxseeds, and ⅓ cup of the sunflower seeds.

4.  Spoon the mixture into the prepared loaf pan, mounding it slightly in the center in a loaf shape.

5.  Scatter the top with the remaining 1 teaspoon flaxseeds and 1 tablespoon sunflower seeds.

6.  Bake until golden brown and a toothpick inserted into the center of the loaf comes out clean, about 45 minutes. Using oven mitts, use the parchment to lift the loaf out of the pan. (Be careful, as it will be very hot: You may want to ask an adult for help!)

7.  Return the parchment and the loaf to the oven without the pan, placing the parchment directly on the center rack.

8.  Bake until the exterior of the loaf is firm and dry, about 8 minutes more. Transfer the bread to a wire rack to cool completely before slicing. Store in a paper bag at room temperature for up to 3 days.

# MOMS SPECIAL GRUYÈRE GRATIN

**Prep time: 10 minutes | Cook time: 20 minutes | serves 8**

4 tablespoons (½ stick) cold unsalted butter, plus 1 tablespoon at room temperature for the baking dish
2 tablespoons extra-virgin olive oil
2 medium yellow onions, thinly sliced
1½ teaspoons kosher salt, divided
Freshly ground black pepper, to taste
2 fennel bulbs, trimmed, halved, cored, and thinly sliced
3 tablespoons cider vinegar
1 (12-inch) loaf crusty Italian bread, cut into ⅓-inch-thick slices and lightly toasted
½ pound (227 g) thinly sliced deli ham
1 tablespoon chopped fresh rosemary
12 ounces (340 g) Gruyère cheese, grated (about 3 cups)
2 cups chicken stock or broth
2 cups heavy cream

1.  Preheat the oven to 425°F(218°C). Use the 1 tablespoon room-temperature butter to grease an oblong 3-quart baking dish.
2.  In a large skillet, melt the remaining 4 tablespoons butter with the oil over medium-low heat. Once the butter has melted, add the onions and 1 teaspoon of the salt.
3.  Cook, stirring occasionally, until the onions are soft and starting to color, 15 to 20 minutes. Season generously with pepper.
4.  Add the fennel and cook, stirring occasionally, until the fennel is soft and the onions are deeply golden, 15 to 20 minutes more. Remove from the heat.
5.  Immediately add the vinegar to the pan and stir to deglaze, using your spoon to scrape up any browned bits from the bottom of the pan. Spoon the onion-fennel mixture into a medium bowl and set aside.
6.  Arrange half the bread slices over the bottom of the prepared baking dish in a single layer, tearing some into smaller pieces if needed to fill any gaps. Spoon half the onion-fennel mixture over the bread in an even layer and lay half the ham slices on top.
7.  Sprinkle half the Gruyère over the ham in an even layer. Repeat the layering with the remaining bread, onion-fennel mixture, ham, and cheese. Sprinkle the top with the rosemary and remaining ½ teaspoon salt, and season with pepper.
8.  In a 4-cup measuring cup, combine the stock and cream. Starting at the edges of the baking dish and slowly working your way toward the center, pour the mixture over the layers of bread and cheese, pausing when needed to let it be absorbed. Continue until the dish is evenly saturated.
9.  Use the back of a spoon or a spatula (or your fingers) to press down on the gratin to compress it. Set aside for about 15 minutes to allow the bread to absorb the cream mixture, pressing it occasionally to compress it a bit more.
10. Cover the dish with foil and place it on a rimmed baking sheet. Bake for 30 minutes, and then remove the foil and bake, uncovered, until the edges are bubbling, the cheese is melted, and the top is golden, about 15 minutes more.
11. Let rest for 15 minutes before serving. Store leftovers, covered, in the refrigerator for up to 3 days.

# HONEYED WHEAT BREAD

Prep time: 10 minutes | Cook time: 20 minutes | makes one 10 inch round loaf

2 cups all-purpose flour, plus more for shaping
2 cups whole wheat flour
2 teaspoons kosher salt
1 teaspoon active dry yeast
2 cups lukewarm water
2 tablespoons honey

1.  In a large bowl, whisk together the all-purpose flour, whole wheat flour, salt, and yeast. In a large measuring cup, combine the lukewarm water and honey and stir until the honey has dissolved.

2.  Pour the honey mixture into the flour mixture and stir with a fork until it forms a wet, sticky dough, about 2 minutes.

3.  Cover the bowl with plastic wrap and set it aside to rest in a warm spot until the dough has doubled in size, at least 18 hours. (One convenient way to time it is to prepare the dough in the afternoon, let the dough rest overnight, and then bake it the following morning.)

4.  When you're ready to bake, place a lidded 6-quart enameled Dutch oven in the oven and preheat the oven to 475°F(246°C). Once the oven is preheated, continue to heat the pan in it for 45 minutes more, until it is scorching hot.

5.  With floured hands, scoop the rested dough from the bowl and place it on a lightly floured large square of parchment paper. At this point the dough should look loose and puffy and contain pockets of small bubbles.

6.  Reflour your hands and lightly shape the dough into a round. Use a sharp knife to make two or three ¼-inch-deep slashes on the top of the loaf.

7.  Carefully remove the Dutch oven from the oven and remove the lid. Always remember to use oven mitts when handling it—or ask a grown-up for help! Holding the edges of the parchment, lift the shaped dough and the parchment together.

8.  Lower them into the Dutch oven so the parchment lines the bottom and the dough sits inside it. Carefully cover the Dutch oven and return it to the oven.

9.  Bake for 30 minutes, then remove the lid and bake until the exterior of the bread is golden and firm and an instant-read thermometer inserted into the center reads 210°F, 15 to 20 minutes more.

# GINGER CAKE WITH WHIPPED CREAM

Prep time: 10 minutes | Cook time: 1 hour 5 minutes | serves 12

3 cups all-purpose flour
2 teaspoons ground ginger
1 teaspoon baking soda
1 teaspoon ground cinnamon
½ teaspoon ground allspice
½ teaspoon ground nutmeg
½ teaspoon salt
¼ teaspoon ground cloves
¼ teaspoon ground black pepper
¾ cup (1½ sticks) butter, softened
1½ cups granulated sugar
1 teaspoon vanilla extract
2 large eggs
1 cup light (mild) molasses
Whipped cream and confectioners' sugar, for garnish

1.  Preheat oven to 350°F(177°C). Grease and flour a 9-inch spring form pan.

2.  In medium bowl with wire whisk, mix flour, ginger, baking soda, cinnamon, allspice, nutmeg, salt, cloves, and pepper.

3.  In large bowl with mixer on medium-high speed, beat butter, granulated sugar, and vanilla for 3 minutes or until creamy, occasionally scraping down side of bowl with rubber spatula.

4.  Reduce speed to medium; add eggs, 1 at a time, beating well after each addition.

5.  In 4-cup measuring cup or medium bowl, stir molasses into 1 cup very hot water. Reduce mixer speed to low. Alternately add flour mixture and molasses, beginning and ending with flour mixture, just until blended.

6.  Pour batter into prepared spring form pan; firmly tap pan against counter to release any bubbles. Bake for 45 to 55 minutes or until toothpick inserted in center of cake comes out clean. Cool cake, in pan, on wire rack for 15 minutes.

7.  With small metal spatula or knife, loosen edges and remove spring form ring. Cool completely.

8.  Cake can be made ahead, wrapped in double layer of plastic wrap, then foil, and frozen for up to 1 month. Thaw in refrigerator.

9.  To serve, top cake with whipped cream and dust with confectioners' sugar.

# ENTICING CHICKEN FILLED BISCUITS BAKE

**Prep time: 10 minutes | Cook time: 20 minutes | serves 6**

FILLING:
2 pounds (907 g) boneless, skinless chicken thighs
2 tablespoons extra-virgin olive oil, divided
Kosher salt and freshly ground black pepper
3 medium golden beets, peeled and diced
4 tablespoons (½ stick) unsalted butter
2 celery stalks, finely diced
1 medium yellow onion, diced
2 large garlic cloves, minced

10 ounces (283 g) white mushrooms, stemmed and thinly sliced
1½ tablespoons chopped fresh thyme
¼ cup all-purpose flour
1¼ cups chicken stock
½ cup half-and-half
½ teaspoon smoked paprika
BISCUITS:
1 tablespoon baking powder
1 teaspoon kosher salt
1 stick (4 ounces (113 g)) unsalted butter, diced
¾ cup heavy cream
¼ cup chopped fresh dill

1. Make the filling: Preheat the oven to 375°F(191°C). Line two baking sheets with parchment paper.

2. Arrange the chicken thighs on one prepared baking sheet.

3. Drizzle with 1 tablespoon of the oil and season with ¼ teaspoon each salt and pepper.

4. Place the beets on the other prepared baking sheet and toss with the remaining 1 tablespoon oil, and season lightly with salt and pepper.

5. Transfer both baking sheets to the oven. Roast the chicken thighs until cooked through, about 25 minutes. Remove the pan from the oven and set aside for about 10 minutes.

6. Roast the beets until tender when pierced with a fork, about 30 minutes. Remove the pan from the oven and set aside. (If you are continuing on to bake the pot pies, leave the oven on, but increase the oven temperature to 425°F(218°C).) When the chicken is cool enough to handle, cut it into coarse chunks and transfer it to a medium bowl, along with any juices from the pan.

7. In a large skillet or Dutch oven, melt the butter over medium heat. Add the celery and onion and sauté until they begin to soften, about 7 minutes.

8. Add the garlic, mushrooms, and thyme and sauté until soft and fragrant, about 5 minutes more. Reduce the heat to medium-low, sprinkle in the flour, and cook, stirring constantly, until the flour is sticky and golden, about 2 minutes.

9. Drizzle in the stock and bring to a simmer. Cook, stirring constantly, until thickened, 1 to 2 minutes.

10. Stir in the half-and-half and smoked paprika and season with salt and pepper. Fold in the chicken and juices and the beets. Remove the pan from the heat and set aside as you prepare the biscuits.

11. Make the biscuits: In a large bowl, whisk together the flour, baking powder, and salt. Use your fingertips to cut the butter into the flour mixture until it is the texture of coarse crumbs and a few pea-size pieces of butter are still visible.

12. Add the cream and dill and stir gently with a fork just until a shaggy dough forms.

13. If you haven't already, preheat the oven to 425°F(218°C). Divide the chicken mixture evenly among six 10-ounce casserole dishes or spoon it into one 9 × 12-inch baking dish.

14. Divide the biscuit batter into 6 portions and scoop it on top of the chicken mixture. If using individual casserole dishes, transfer them to a rimmed baking sheet.

15. Bake until the filling is bubbling at the edges and the biscuits are puffed and golden, 20 to 25 minutes. Let rest for 5 minutes before serving.

# VANILLA FROSTED MARSHMALLOWS COOKIES

**Prep time: 10 minutes | Cook time: 1 hour 15 minutes | makes 3 dozen cookies**

Vanilla Sugar Cookie Dough
Red food coloring
2 cans (16 ounces (170 g) each) vanilla frosting

Mini marshmallows
Pink M&M's
Pink candy-coated sunflower seeds

1. Prepare Vanilla Sugar Cookie Dough as directed for cutouts. With floured 3-inch-round cutter, cut out rounds for bodies. With floured 1-inch, egg-shaped cutter, cut out ovals for feet. Bake as directed.

2. With red food coloring, tint 1 can of frosting pink.

3. To assemble, spread white and pink frosting on cooled cookie rounds and ovals. Press ovals into edges of rounds; press marshmallows into centers for tails.

4. Place M&M's in middle of feet and candy-coated sunflower seeds on edges of feet for toes. Let cookies stand for about 2 hours or until frosting is set.

# VANILLA BERRY MUFFINS

**Prep time: 10 minutes | Cook time: 45 minutes | Makes 12 muffins**

1 ⅓ cups all-purpose flour
½ teaspoon baking powder
½ teaspoon baking soda
¾ cup granulated white sugar
½ cup grape seed oil
½ teaspoon vanilla extract
½ teaspoon salt
1 large egg
⅓ cup milk
1 ¼ cups berries, such as blueberries, blackberries, and raspberries
BAKING EQUIPMENT
Measuring cups and spoons
Cupcake tin
Cupcake liners
Nonstick cooking spray
Sifter
2 mixing bowls
Electric hand mixer
Rubber spatula
Oven-safe gloves

1. Preheat your oven to 400°F(204°C). Line your cupcake tin with cupcake liners, then spray the liners with cooking spray.

2. Sift together the flour, baking powder, and baking soda into a mixing bowl.

3. Using an electric hand mixer in another mixing bowl, mix together the sugar, oil, vanilla, and salt on medium speed for 1 minute.

4. Add the egg and milk. Mix for 1 minute.

5. Add the flour mixture into the liquid mixture. Mix until incorporated.

6. Turn off the mixer. Using a spatula, fold your berries into the batter.

7. Scoop your batter into the prepared cupcake tin. Fill only two-thirds full because the batter will expand.

8. Put the cupcake tin in the oven. Bake for 20 minutes, or until a toothpick inserted into the center of a muffin comes out clean.

9. Using oven-safe gloves, remove the tin from the oven. Let the cupcakes cool for 20 minutes. Remove the cupcakes from the tin. Leftover muffins can be stored in an airtight container at room temperature for up to 2 days.

TIP: Berries naturally start to sink to the bottom of muffins because they are heavy. However, if you dust them with flour before folding them into the batter, it will help them float.

# CHEESY TOMATO ITALIAN BREAD

**Prep time: 10 minutes | Cook time: 20 minutes | serves 8**

4¼ cups all-purpose flour
1 tablespoon kosher salt, plus more for seasoning
2½ teaspoons instant yeast
1¾ cups warm water
5 tablespoons extra-virgin olive oil, divided, plus more for the bowl
2 pints multicolored cherry tomatoes, halved (about 3½ cups)
8 large eggs
1 cup finely grated Parmesan cheese
Freshly ground black pepper, to taste
1 tablespoon chopped fresh chives

1. In a food processor, pulse together the flour, salt, and yeast. Add the water and 2 tablespoons of the oil and pulse until a rough ball of dough forms, about 1 minute. The dough will be sticky.

2. Using a rubber spatula, transfer the dough to a clean work surface. Shape the dough into a ball; place it in a lightly oiled large bowl, and turn to coat the dough with oil.

3. Cover the bowl with plastic wrap and let rest at room temperature until doubled in size, 1½ to 2 hours.

4. Drizzle the remaining 3 tablespoons oil onto a rimmed baking sheet. Punch down the dough and transfer it to the baking sheet, turning it to coat with oil. Stretch the dough to the edges of the baking sheet.

5. Lightly cover the baking sheet with plastic wrap and let sit at room temperature until nearly doubled in size again, 1 to 1½ hours.

6. Position a rack in the center of the oven and preheat the oven to 450°F(232°C).

7. Use your fingertips to press 8 evenly spaced wells across the dough (these will hold the eggs later). Scatter the tomatoes over the dough (avoiding the wells) and season with salt.

8. Bake the focaccia until the edges are lightly golden brown, 20 to 25 minutes. Remove from the oven.

9. Crack an egg into a small bowl, then carefully add it to one of the wells. Repeat with the remaining eggs.

10. Sprinkle with Parmesan and season with pepper. Bake until the egg whites are just set and the yolks are soft, 8 to 10 minutes.

11. Garnish with the chives. Let rest for 2 minutes in the pan, then slice into squares with a pizza cutter and serve.

# CHAPTER 7: HEALTHY SALADS AND VEGGIES

# MIXED CABBAGE SLAW WITH SANDWICHES

Prep time: 10 minutes | Cook time: 0 minutes | serves 4

4 tablespoons olive oil
3 tablespoons fish sauce
1 tablespoon sherry vinegar
Juice of 1 lime
1 teaspoon brown sugar
Flake salt, such as Maldon
½ head red cabbage
½ head green cabbage
Freshly ground black pepper, to taste
TOOLS / EQUIPMENT:
Citrus reamer
Small bowl
Whisk
Large bowl

1. Make the dressing. In a small bowl, combine the olive oil, fish sauce, vinegar, lime juice, sugar, and a small pinch of salt, whisking vigorously to dissolve the sugar. Taste, adjust seasoning as needed, and set aside.

2. Make the slaw. With the flat side of the cabbage flush against your cutting board, use a very sharp knife to slice the cabbage very thinly and transfer to a large bowl.

3. Use two forks to toss half the dressing in with the cabbage mix. Add the remainder, and toss again to coat. Season with pepper.

4. Serve. The slaw is best once the acids in the dressing soften the crunchy cabbage slightly, at least 20 minutes. Before serving, toss the slaw to reincorporate the dressing accumulated at the bottom of the bowl, then pile the slaw onto sandwiches or serve as a super-flavorful, crunchy side. Keeps in the refrigerator, covered, for 1 week.

# CUCUMBER SALAD WITH GRILLED MEAT

Prep time: 10 minutes | Cook time: 3 minutes | serves 4

3 tablespoons rice wine vinegar
1 tablespoon toasted sesame oil
1 tablespoon soy sauce
½ teaspoon sugar
4 cups Persian, hothouse, or other thin-skinned cucumbers, scrubbed and chopped
2 scallions, ends trimmed and sliced thin on a diagonal
⅓ cup chopped fresh cilantro
Pinch flake salt, such as Maldon
1 tablespoon sesame seeds
Delicious additions:
Minced pickled or fresh ginger
Minced garlic
Red pepper flakes
Bonito flakes
TOOLS / EQUIPMENT
Medium bowl
Whisk
Small skillet

1. Make the dressing. In a medium bowl, whisk to combine the rice wine vinegar, sesame oil, soy sauce, and sugar, dissolving the sugar.

2. Compose the salad. Add the cucumbers, scallions, cilantro, and salt, and toss to coat well. Taste and adjust seasoning as necessary. Allow the salad to sit for at least 10 minutes for the flavors to meld.

3. Toast the seeds. In a small dry skillet over medium heat, toast the sesame seeds until golden, about 3 minutes.

4. Serve. Serve chilled with the toasted sesame seeds sprinkled on top. Pairs well with grilled meats, seared fish or shrimp, brown rice, or broiled, marinated tofu.

# CITRUSY AVOCADO MELON BALLS

## Prep time: 15 minutes | Cook time: 10 minutes | serves 4

$\frac{1}{3}$ cup plus 1 tablespoon olive oil, divided
2 limes, one juiced and one cut into wedges for serving
$\frac{1}{4}$ cup chopped fresh mint
Sea salt, to taste
Freshly ground black pepper, to taste
1 (8-ounce/226 g) block Haloumi

cheese, sliced into $\frac{1}{4}$-inch slices
1 cantaloupe, halved and seeded
2 avocados, halved and pitted
**TOOLS / EQUIPMENT**
Citrus reamer
Small bowl
Small cast-iron skillet
Metal spatula
Melon baller

1.  Make the dressing. In a small bowl, stir together $\frac{1}{3}$ cup of olive oil with the juice of 1 lime, mint, and salt and pepper to taste. Set aside.

2.  Fry the cheese. In a small cast-iron skillet over medium-high heat, heat the remaining 1 tablespoon of olive oil. Add the cheese slices, and lower the heat to medium.

3.  Moisture from the cheese can cause the oil to spatter, so be careful as you lay them in. Sear the cheese for a few minutes—you should hear them sizzle.

4.  Flip to the second side when the first is caramelized and browned. The second side takes only a couple minutes. Transfer to a serving platter.

5.  Prepare the melon. Use a melon baller to make spheres from the cantaloupe's flesh, and then arrange them on the platter beside the Haloumi.

6.  Prepare the avocado. Repeat the process with the avocados. Do this just before serving time so that the avocado doesn't oxidize, and squeeze a wedge or two of fresh lime juice over the avocado spheres, tossing to coat.

7.  Serve. Layer the mixture of avocado and melon balls next to the Haloumi, and spoon the chopped mint dressing over all. Serve with the remaining lime wedges, and eat immediately.

# WATERMELON SWEET CORN SALAD

## Prep time: 15 minutes | Cook time: 0 minutes | serves 4

5 fresh basil leaves
$\frac{1}{2}$ small watermelon, seeded, rind removed, cut into 1-inch cubes
2 ears fresh sweet corn, cooked and cut off cob

1 teaspoon ground sumac
$\frac{1}{4}$ teaspoon ground cayenne
Zest of $\frac{1}{2}$ lemon
Flake salt, such as Maldon
**TOOLS / EQUIPMENT**
Zester

1.  Transfer the cubed watermelon and any accumulated juices to a serving platter.

2.  Add the corn cut off the cobs (it is okay if there are rows of corn left intact; that is part of the fun). Sprinkle the sumac and cayenne over the mixture, followed by the lemon zest.

3.  Cut the basil into a chiffonade. Do this immediately prior to serving the salad, as the edges

of the basil will darken from being cut (known as oxidation). Stack the basil leaves on top of each other, and roll into a tight bundle.

4.  Slice your knife across the roll, creating very thin strips (called chiffonade). Fluff the chiffonade to separate the strips, and scatter onto the salad.

5.  Serve. Season with salt, and serve immediately.

# POTATO DILL SPRIGS SALAD

## Prep time: 10 minutes | Cook time: 10 minutes | serves 4

6 medium Yukon gold potatoes, scrubbed and cut into chunky wedges
3 medium Red Bliss potatoes, scrubbed and cut into chunky wedges
4 to 5 tablespoons olive oil
2 tablespoons whole-grain mustard
1 tablespoon capers, well-rinsed

and chopped
1 shallot, sliced thin
3 tablespoons dill, torn into small sprigs
Sea salt and freshly ground black pepper, to taste
**TOOLS / EQUIPMENT**
Large saucepan
Colander
Large bowl
Boil the potatoes.

1.  In a large saucepan, cover the potatoes with water and gently boil them for 8 to 10 minutes, until fork-tender. Drain the potatoes in a colander, and transfer to a large bowl.

2.  Dress the potatoes. In a large bowl, toss the olive

oil, mustard, capers, and shallot to combine with the potatoes.

3.  Serve. Once the potato mixture has cooled to room temperature, add the dill sprigs, and toss again. Season to taste with salt and pepper. Enjoy warm, at room temperature, or chilled.

# CHEESY HAZELNUT KALE SALAD

**Prep time: 15 minutes | Cook time: 10 minutes | serves 4**

1 bunch lacinato kale, also known as Tuscan or dinosaur kale, rinsed, ends trimmed
Zest and juice of 1 lemon
2 tablespoons olive oil
Flake salt, such as Maldon
Freshly ground black pepper, to taste
1 cup hazelnuts
½ cup shaved Parmigiano-Reggiano
TOOLS / EQUIPMENT
Citrus reamer
Zester
Vegetable peeler
Large bowl
Baking sheet
Toaster oven
Small serving bowl

1.  Chop the kale. Gather the kale into a tight bunch or stack the leaves on top of each other, and slice into very thin strips, about ⅛ inch wide. Transfer to a large bowl.

2.  Dress the salad. Add the lemon zest and juice and the olive oil to the bowl, season with salt and pepper, and toss to combine. Taste and adjust seasoning, and set aside.

3.  Prepare the nuts. Toast the hazelnuts for 5 minutes or until fragrant. When cool enough to handle, gently rub off their skins. Arrange the nuts on a cutting board.

4.  Coarsely crush them by leaning your weight onto the side of a chef's knife placed on them. Transfer nuts to the toaster oven tray and toast again until golden, about 3 minutes more. Empty the nuts into a small serving bowl.

5.  Serve. At the table, scatter the hazelnuts and shaved Parm over the salad, and serve immediately.

Tip: Chopping and dressing the kale can be done a day in advance, giving time for the citrus to break down the leaves' sturdiness. If you do make it ahead, toss again before adding final toppings to redistribute the dressing.

# TOMATO SALAD WITH SALT AND PEPPER

**Prep time: 10 minutes | Cook time: 10 minutes | serves 4**

1 loaf crusty bread, torn into bite-size chunks and left to dry out on a baking sheet for 1 to 2 days
2 tablespoons olive oil, plus extra for soaking, drizzling, and frying
Flake salt, such as Maldon
Freshly ground black pepper, to taste
5 large heirloom tomatoes, cut into wedges
1½ cups Sun Gold tomatoes, halved
2 cups fresh basil leaves, rinsed and patted dry
4 chives, finely chopped
2 teaspoons red wine vinegar
TOOLS / EQUIPMENT
Bread knife
Baking sheet
Small bowl
Whisk

1.  Preheat the oven to 425°F(218°C). Toast the bread.

2.  Arrange the bread on a baking sheet, and drizzle with olive oil, and season with salt and pepper. Toast the bread in the oven until golden and crisp on the edges, turning once halfway through as needed, about 8 minutes total.

3.  Assemble the salad.

4.  Arrange the tomatoes on a serving platter, alternating shapes and colors. Add the basil, and nestle the crispy bread into the mixture, then scatter the chives all around.

5.  Make the dressing. In a small bowl, whisk the olive oil and red wine vinegar to combine.

6.  Drizzle the dressing over the salad, saving some for at the table, season with salt and pepper, and dig in.

# TUNA TOMATO AND OLIVE SALAD

**Prep time: 10 minutes | Cook time: 7 minutes | serves 4**

FOR THE DRESSING
½ cup olive oil
2 tablespoons white wine vinegar
1 teaspoon Dijon mustard
1 small shallot, minced
3 tablespoons finely chopped fresh parsley
Kosher salt and Freshly ground black pepper, to taste
FOR THE SALAD
4 eggs, cold
Ice water
5 potatoes, peeled and boiled until fork tender
2 handfuls very fresh haricots verts, scrubbed, stem ends trimmed
1 head romaine, Bibb lettuce, or arugula, leaves rinsed and patted dry
5 radishes, sliced into thin wedges
½ cup pitted Niçoise (or other oil-cured) olives

1 lemon, sliced into rounds
2 cans oil-packed tuna, drained
2 tablespoons finely chopped chives or thinly sliced red onion
1 tablespoon capers, rinsed
6 anchovies (optional)
Delicious additions
Cooked artichoke hearts
Steamed asparagus
Cherry tomatoes or tomato wedges
Marinated beets
TOOLS / EQUIPMENT
Paring knife
Vegetable peeler
Small bowl
Whisk
Large saucepan
Large
slotted spoon
Large bowl
Colander

To make the dressing:

1. In a small bowl, whisk to combine the olive oil, vinegar, mustard, shallot, and parsley. Season with salt and pepper, and set aside.

2. Boil the eggs. In a saucepan large enough to fit the eggs in a single layer, add enough water to cover them by 1 inch, and bring the water to a boil. Use a large spoon to carefully lower refrigerator-cold eggs into the water, one at a time, and return to a simmer, adjusting heat as necessary.

3. Simmer for 6 minutes for a liquid-gold yolk, 7 to 9 minutes for a custardy yolk. After your preferred cook time, use a slotted spoon to transfer the eggs to a large bowl filled with ice water.

4. Peel the eggs. Once the eggs are cool enough to handle, tap them on the counter to crack the shells all over, and carefully peel them. Rinse each briefly under

cold water to remove any stray shell bits, then quarter them.

5. Cut the potatoes. Once they are cool enough to handle, slice potatoes into bite-sized wedges and set aside.

6. Cut the haricots verts. Stack the haricots verts and slice them into bite-size pieces on a sharp diagonal.

7. Assemble the salad and serve. On a serving platter, arrange salad leaves to cover. Stack the quartered eggs, haricots verts, sliced radishes, olives, lemon wheels, and boiled potatoes into piles or rows, alongside the chunks of tuna.

8. Scatter the chives and capers over everything, add the anchovies (if using) piled either in the center or laid out over the other elements, and spoon the dressing over all. Serve immediately.

# HONEYED CARROTS BAKE

**Prep time: 10 minutes | Cook time: 35 minutes | serves 4**

2 tablespoons butter
2 tablespoons honey
Flake salt, such as Maldon
2 to 3 bunches small carrots, scrubbed and greens trimmed, halved lengthwise if thick
2 fresh rosemary sprigs, quills stripped from stems and

coarsely chopped
Freshly ground black pepper, to taste
TOOLS / EQUIPMENT
Small saucepan
Whisk
Baking sheet
Rubber spatula

1. Preheat the oven to 425°F(218°C). Prepare the glaze.

2. In a small saucepan over medium heat, melt the butter. Add the honey, and whisk to dissolve. Season with a pinch of salt, and set aside.

3. Toss the ingredients together. On a baking sheet, drizzle the honey mixture over the carrots, toss to coat, and scatter the chopped rosemary on top. Season with

salt and pepper.

4. Roast the carrots.

5. Bake for 30 to 35 minutes, or until the carrots are tender and caramelized in spots, rearranging them for even browning halfway through.

6. Serve. Transfer to a serving platter or plates and eat warm.

# CITRUSY MAYO EGG SALAD

Prep time: 10 minutes | Cook time: 15 minutes | serves 4

8 eggs
Ice water
4 slices crusty bread, such as sourdough or seeded wheat, crusts removed, and cut diagonally in half, into triangles
2 tablespoons mayonnaise
2 teaspoons Dijon mustard
1 teaspoon freshly squeezed lemon juice
1 celery stalk, finely chopped
1 tablespoon finely chopped cornichons
1 tablespoon finely chopped parsley
Sea salt, to taste
Freshly ground black pepper, to taste

TOOLS / EQUIPMENT
Citrus reamer
Large saucepan
Large bowl
Large
slotted spoon
Toaster oven
Medium bowl

1. Cook the eggs. In a saucepan large enough for the eggs to sit in a single layer, bring to a boil enough water to submerge the eggs by at least 1 inch. Carefully lower the eggs into the water, return to a boil, and simmer for 10 minutes. Have a large bowl filled with ice water nearby.

2. Transfer and peel the eggs.

3. Use a slotted spoon to transfer the eggs to the water to chill them for peeling. Let the eggs sit in the ice bath until cool to the touch. Tap the eggshell on your work surface, turning it and cracking it throughout. Peel the shells and discard.

4. Toast the bread pieces in the toaster oven until golden and crisp. Transfer to individual plates or a serving dish.

5. Assemble the salad. In a medium bowl, use a fork or potato masher to mash the hard-cooked eggs, combining them with the mayonnaise, mustard, and lemon juice. You may opt to keep the consistency chunky, or for a creamier consistency, mash until well combined.

6. Finish assembling. Add the celery, cornichons, and parsley, and season with salt and pepper. Stir gently to combine.

7. Serve with the toast points chilled or at room temperature. Any leftovers will keep, sealed in the refrigerator, for up to 4 days.

# CITRUSY AVOCADO MELON BALLS

Prep time: 15 minutes | Cook time: 10 minutes | serves 4

⅓ cup plus 1 tablespoon olive oil, divided
2 limes, one juiced and one cut into wedges for serving
¼ cup chopped fresh mint
Sea salt, to taste
Freshly ground black pepper, to taste
1 (8-ounce/226 g) block Haloumi cheese, sliced into ¼-inch slices
1 cantaloupe, halved and seeded
2 avocados, halved and pitted

TOOLS / EQUIPMENT
Citrus reamer
Small bowl
Small cast-iron skillet
Metal spatula
Melon baller

1. Make the dressing. In a small bowl, stir together ⅓ cup of olive oil with the juice of 1 lime, mint, and salt and pepper to taste. Set aside.

2. Fry the cheese. In a small cast-iron skillet over medium-high heat, heat the remaining 1 tablespoon of olive oil. Add the cheese slices, and lower the heat to medium.

3. Moisture from the cheese can cause the oil to spatter, so be careful as you lay them in. Sear the cheese for a few minutes—you should hear them sizzle.

4. Flip to the second side when the first is caramelized and browned. The second side takes only a couple minutes. Transfer to a serving platter.

5. Prepare the melon. Use a melon baller to make spheres from the cantaloupe's flesh, and then arrange them on the platter beside the Haloumi.

6. Prepare the avocado. Repeat the process with the avocados. Do this just before serving time so that the avocado doesn't oxidize, and squeeze a wedge or two of fresh lime juice over the avocado spheres, tossing to coat.

7. Serve. Layer the mixture of avocado and melon balls next to the Haloumi, and spoon the chopped mint dressing over all. Serve with the remaining lime wedges, and eat immediately.

# ONE PAN ROASTED CAULIFLOWER

**Prep time: 10 minutes | Cook time: 35 minutes | serves 4**

FOR THE CAULIFLOWER
1½ cups dry white wine or white wine vinegar
6 cups water
⅓ cup olive oil, plus more for serving
3 tablespoons kosher salt
3 tablespoons freshly squeezed lemon juice
2 tablespoons orange juice
2 tablespoons butter
1 tablespoon crushed red pepper flakes
Pinch black peppercorns
1 bay leaf
1 head cauliflower, stem trimmed
Flake salt, such as Maldon, for serving

FOR THE SAUCE
½ cup crème fraîche
3 tablespoons nonfat Greek yogurt
¼ cup finely shredded Parmigiano-Reggiano
3 teaspoons capers, rinsed and chopped
Freshly ground black pepper, to taste

TOOLS / EQUIPMENT
Citrus reamer
Box grater
Dutch oven
Rubber spatula
Small bowl
Roasting pan

1. Poach the cauliflower. In a Dutch oven or other heavy-bottomed pot over high heat, bring the wine, water, olive oil, kosher salt, lemon juice, orange juice, butter, red pepper flakes, peppercorns, and bay leaf to a boil.

2. Add the cauliflower, and then reduce the heat to simmer. Turn occasionally, using a pair of serving spoons to submerge each side in the poaching liquid, until a knife easily inserts into center, 15 to 20 minutes.

3. Preheat the oven to 475°F(246°C).

4. Make the dipping sauce. In a small bowl, mix together the crème fraîche, Greek yogurt, cheese, and capers, and season with pepper. Set aside.

5. Roast the cauliflower. Using tongs or the serving spoons, transfer cauliflower to a roasting pan. Roast, rotating the sheet if browning unevenly, until deep golden and crispy in parts, about 35 minutes.

6. Serve. Bring the roasted cauliflower to the table, set on a trivet, and serve directly from the roasting pan with the dipping sauce—and a spoon to dispense it—alongside.

# ROASTED BRUSSELS SPROUTS AND SHALLOTS

**Prep time: 10 minutes | Cook time: 30 minutes | serves 4**

1½ pounds Brussels sprouts, trimmed and halved
6 shallots, quartered
3 tablespoons olive oil
Sea salt, to taste
Freshly ground black pepper, to taste
1 lemon, cut into wedges, for serving

TOOLS / EQUIPMENT
2 baking sheets
Tongs

1. Arrange oven racks and preheat oven. Place one oven rack in the top third of the oven and another in the bottom third, then preheat oven to 450°F(232°C).

2. Prep the veggie mixture. On two baking sheets, toss the Brussels sprouts and shallots with the olive oil, placing most of the Brussels halves cut-side down. Season with salt and pepper.

3. Roast the vegetables. Swap the pans halfway through, and use tongs to turn the veggies over for even roasting. Cook until caramelized and tender, 25 to 30 minutes.

4. Serve. Transfer the Brussels sprouts and shallots to a serving dish, with lemon wedges to squeeze at the table.

# HEALTHY RAINBOW SALAD

**Prep time: 15 minutes | Cook time: 5 minutes | serves 4**

4 red, orange, and yellow bell peppers, cored and sliced into thin, bite-size strips
2 celery stalks, diced
1 handful green beans, ends trimmed, sliced into thin coins
¼ cup chopped fresh parsley
2 tablespoons capers, rinsed and chopped
2 tablespoons olive oil
2 teaspoons sherry or champagne vinegar
Freshly ground black pepper, to taste
⅓ cup slivered almonds

TOOLS / EQUIPMENT
Toaster oven

1. Toast the nuts. Arrange almonds in a single layer on a toaster oven tray. Toast for 4 minutes, or until they become fragrant and their edges turn golden. You may agitate pan halfway through, circulating the almonds for even toasting. Transfer them to a small dish.

2. Assemble the salad. Layer the peppers, celery, green beans, parsley, and capers onto a serving platter. Toss slightly to incorporate.

3. Serve. Drizzle the salad with the olive oil and vinegar, season with pepper, and scatter the toasted almonds on top. Serve immediately.

# ROASTED SQUASH RINGS

Prep time: 15 minutes | Cook time: 30 minutes | serves 4

3 delicata squash, halved widthwise
Olive oil, for drizzling
Flake salt, such as Maldon
Freshly ground black pepper
TOOLS / EQUIPMENT
Pointy teaspoon
2 baking sheets
Metal spatula

1. Arrange oven racks and preheat oven. Place one oven rack in the top third of the oven and another in the bottom third, then preheat oven to 425°F(218°C).

2. Prepare the squash. Use a pointy teaspoon to scrape the seeds and any stringy bits from each squash half and discard (or save for compost). Slice the squash into ½-inch rings, discarding the stem ends.

3. Prep the squash for roasting. Drizzle 1 to 2 tablespoons of olive oil onto each baking sheet, and spread it around with your fingers to coat the pans. Lay the delicata rings flat in a single layer on each sheet, and lightly drizzle with olive oil. Season with salt and pepper.

4. Roast the squash. Cook for 10 to 15 minutes, until the rings begin to brown on the bottom, then the flip rings to the other side, season again, and swap the pans, returning them to roast for another 10 to 15 minutes, until the squash is tender and deeply golden in spots. Test by seeing if you can pierce them with a fork— if you can, they are ready.

5. Serve warm for a delicious snack or side dish.

# BUTTERMILK DRESSING IN LETTUCE WEDGES

Prep time: 10 minutes | Cook time: 0 minutes | serves 4

½ cup buttermilk
2 to 3 tablespoons sour cream
1 teaspoon Dijon mustard
1 tablespoon apple cider vinegar
2 tablespoons chopped fresh chives, tarragon, dill, or parsley, or a combination
1 garlic clove, finely grated
Few dashes hot sauce
¼ teaspoon freshly ground black pepper
Pinch flake salt, such as Maldon
3 heads lettuce (such as gem, Bibb, or butter), root ends trimmed and quartered lengthwise
TOOLS / EQUIPMENT
Fine grater
Mason jar with lid

1. Make the dressing. In a mason jar with a lid, combine the buttermilk, sour cream, mustard, vinegar, chives, garlic, hot sauce, pepper, and salt. Close it tightly, then shake it like crazy. After 30 seconds to a minute of vigorous shaking, open the jar and taste, adjust the seasonings as needed, seal, and shake again.

2. Serve.

3. Divide the lettuce wedges and herbs evenly onto plates. Spoon the dressing directly from the mason jar onto the greens. Sprinkle salt and pepper to taste. Any remaining dressing will keep sealed, in the refrigerator, for up to 5 days. You'll want to use it on everything: roasted potatoes, carrot spears, roast chicken, and more!

# CHAPTER 8: DINNER

# EASY SAVORY DIP WITH PITA CHIPS

**Prep time: 10 minutes | Cook time: 5 minutes | serves 6**

FOR THE HUMMUS
1½ cups shelled edamame
2 garlic cloves or 1 tablespoon garlic paste
⅓ cup sesame oil (tahini)
¼ cup packed cilantro leaves
½ cup water
¼ cup freshly squeezed lemon juice
¼ cup olive oil
½ teaspoon ground cumin
½ teaspoon kosher salt
FOR SERVING
Pita chips, carrots, and celery
TOOLS/EQUIPMENT
Small pot
Colander or strainer
Food processor
Rubber or silicone spatula
Serving bowl

1.  Cook the edamame. In a small pot of salted water, boil the edamame until tender, 5 to 6 minutes. Drain in a colander, and rinse with cold water to cool. Set aside.
2.  Blend and serve.
3.  In a food processor, pulse the garlic until minced. Add the edamame and the remaining hummus ingredients, and process until smooth. Use a rubber or silicone spatula to transfer to a serving bowl, and serve with pita chips, carrots, and celery.

# GOLDEN CRISP CHEESE BAKE

**Prep time: 10 minutes | Cook time: 25 minutes | serves 4**

½ cup water
4 tablespoons butter
Pinch salt
½ cup all-purpose flour
Pinch freshly ground black pepper
1 large egg, plus 1 large egg white
½ cup grated extra-sharp Cheddar cheese
TOOLS/EQUIPMENT
Grater
Baking sheet
Parchment paper
Medium saucepan
Wooden spoon or rubber spatula
Medium bowl

1.  Preheat the oven. Preheat the oven to 400°F(204°C), and line a baking sheet with parchment paper.
2.  Melt the butter.
3.  In a medium saucepan, bring the water, butter, and salt to a simmer. When the butter has melted, remove the pan from the heat.
4.  Add the flour and pepper. Mix vigorously with a wooden spoon or rubber spatula until it forms thick dough.
5.  Add the eggs and cheese.
6.  Transfer the dough to a medium bowl. Using the spoon or a mixer, add the egg and then the egg white, continuing to mix until fully incorporated. Allow the dough to cool to just slightly warm, then mix in the cheese.
7.  Bake the puffs.
8.  Spoon 1-inch pieces of dough onto the baking sheet about 1 inch apart. Bake until golden and crisp, about 25 minutes. Serve warm.

# PRETZEL BAKE WITH HONEYED DIP

## Prep time: 10 minutes | Cook time: 17 minutes | serves 24

**FOR THE PRETZELS**
1½ cups warm water (115°F/46°C)
1 tablespoon granulated sugar
1 (¼-ounce) envelope active dry yeast
4 to 4½ cups all-purpose flour, plus more to flour the work surface
2 teaspoons table salt
4 tablespoons unsalted butter, melted
1 tablespoon vegetable or canola oil
Butter, for greasing the baking sheets (optional)
**FOR THE WATER BATH AND TOPPING**
8 cups water
½ cup baking soda
1 egg yolk
1 to 2 teaspoons pretzel salt or coarse salt
**FOR THE HONEY MUSTARD DIP**
½ cup mayonnaise
¼ cup honey
¼ cup yellow mustard
**TOOLS/EQUIPMENT:**
Stand mixer or large bowl
Large gowl
2 baking sheets
Parchment paper (optional)
Large saucepan
Slotted spoon
Pastry brush
Wire rack
Small bowl

1. Prepare the yeast. In the bowl of a stand mixer with the hook attachment on, stir together 1½ cups of warm water, sugar, and yeast until blended, then let it sit for about 5 minutes.

2. Blend the ingredients. Add about 3½ cups of flour, the salt, and melted butter to the bowl. Mix on low with the hook attachment until well blended.

3. Add more flour as needed for the dough to come together. Raise the speed to medium, and continue kneading for 4 to 6 minutes or until dough is smooth and elastic.

4. Let the dough rise. Grease a large bowl with the oil, add the dough, turn it to coat, cover with plastic wrap and place in a warm, draft-free place to double in size, about 1 hour.

5. Preheat the oven to 450°F(232°C).

6. Generously grease 2 baking sheets or line with parchment paper. Prepare the water bath.

7. In a large saucepan over high heat, add the 8 cups of water and baking soda. Bring to a boil, and stir to blend.

8. Form the pretzel sticks.

9. While waiting for the water to boil, place the risen dough on a lightly floured surface. Divide the dough in half, and then divide each half into 12 balls, for a total of 24 balls. Roll out each ball into a rope 4 to 5 inches long. Dust off any excess flour from the pretzels.

10. Put the pretzels in the water bath.

11. Gently lower each pretzel into the boiling water, 2 or 3 at a time, and cook for 20 to 30 seconds. Remove the pretzels with a large slotted spoon or spatula, gently shaking off any excess water, then place the pretzels on the baking sheets.

12. Mix the egg yolk with a little water to thin in a small bowl. With a pastry brush, lightly brush the egg yolk on top of the pretzels, then sprinkle with the pretzel or coarse salt.

13. Bake the pretzels. Bake for 12 to 17 minutes, or until dark golden brown. Cool slightly, and then transfer the pretzels to a wire rack to finish cooling before serving.

14. Make the honey mustard dip. In a small bowl, mix together the mayonnaise, honey, and mustard, and serve alongside the pretzels.

# CHEESY MUFFIN WITH PIZZA SAUCE

## Prep time: 10 minutes | Cook time: 15 minutes | serves 6

**FOR THE BITES**
Nonstick cooking spray
1 cup all-purpose flour
1 cup shredded mozzarella
1 cup chopped pepperoni slices
1 cup whole milk
1 large egg
1 teaspoon baking powder
**FOR SERVING**
Pizza sauce, for dipping
**TOOLS/EQUIPMENT**
Cutting board
Knife
Mini muffin pan
Large bowl
Rubber or silicone spatula
Toothpick

1. Preheat the oven. Preheat the oven to 375°F(191°C). Spray the cups of a mini muffin pan with cooking spray.

2. Mix, fill, and bake. In a large bowl, combine all the pizza bites ingredients and mix with a rubber spatula until blended. Fill each muffin cup three-quarters full with batter.

3. Bake for 12 to 14 minutes, or until puffed and a toothpick inserted into a muffin comes out clean. Serve with pizza sauce for dipping.

# HONEYED MUFFIN WITH BUTTERY ORANGE

**Prep time: 10 minutes | Cook time: 17 minutes | makes 18 muffins**

FOR THE MUFFINS
Butter, for greasing the pans (optional)
Flour, for dusting the pans (optional)
1 cup all-purpose flour
1 cup yellow cornmeal
½ cup granulated sugar
1 tablespoon baking powder
1 teaspoon table salt
1 cup milk (2 percent or whole)
½ cup (1 stick) unsalted butter, melted and cooled
¼ cup honey
2 large eggs, at room temperature
FOR THE ORANGE HONEY BUTTER
½ cup (1 stick) unsalted butter, at room temperature
¼ teaspoon table salt
2 tablespoons honey
1 teaspoon freshly grated orange zest
1 teaspoon freshly squeezed orange juice
TOOLS/EQUIPMENT:
 2 muffin pans
 Paper liners (optional)
 Large bowl
 Medium bowl
 Zester
 Small bowl

1. Preheat the oven to 400°F (204°C).
2. Generously grease and lightly flour 18 cups of 2 (12-cup) muffin pans, or line the pans with paper liners.
3. Mix the dry ingredients.
4. In a large bowl, mix together the flour, cornmeal, sugar, baking powder, and 1 teaspoon of salt.
5. Mix the wet ingredients.
6. In a medium bowl, mix together the milk, ½ cup of melted butter, ¼ cup of honey, and the eggs until well combined.
7. Blend the ingredients.
8. Make a well in the middle of the dry ingredients, and pour the wet ingredients into the middle. Mix until just combined.
9. Bake the muffins.
10. Spoon the batter into the prepared pans. Bake for 14 to 17 minutes or until a toothpick inserted into the middle of a muffin comes out clean.
11. Make the orange honey butter.
12. Meanwhile, in a small bowl, mix together the ½ cup of room-temperature butter, ¼ teaspoon of salt, 2 tablespoons of honey, orange zest, and orange juice until well combined. Serve with the warm muffins.

# CHEESE CAKE DRIZZLED BLUEBERRY MUFFIN

**Prep time: 10 minutes | Cook time: 14 minutes | makes 24 muffins**

FOR THE MUFFIN TOPS
Butter, for greasing the baking sheets (optional)
1½ cups all-purpose flour
¾ cup granulated sugar
1½ teaspoons baking powder
½ teaspoon table salt
⅓ cup milk (2 percent or whole)
⅓ cup vegetable or canola oil
1 large egg plus 1 large egg yolk
1 teaspoon vanilla extract
2 cups fresh blueberries
FOR THE CHEESECAKE DRIZZLE
4 ounces (113 g) cream cheese, at room temperature
½ cup confectioners' sugar
¼ teaspoon vanilla extract
3 to 5 tablespoons milk (2 percent or whole)
TOOLS/EQUIPMENT:
2 baking sheets
Parchment paper (optional)
2 medium bowls
Whisk
Small bowl
Wire rack

1. Preheat the oven to 375°F. Grease 2 large baking sheets, or line with parchment paper.
2. Mix the dry ingredients.
3. In a medium bowl, stir together the flour, granulated sugar, baking powder, and salt.
4. Mix the wet ingredients.
5. In another medium bowl, whisk together the ⅓ cup of milk, oil, egg and egg yolk, and 1 teaspoon vanilla until well combined.
6. Combine the ingredients.
7. Make a well in the center of the dry ingredients. Add the wet ingredients to the middle of the dry ingredients, and stir until nearly blended. Some lumps are okay. Gently fold in the blueberries until everything is just combined.
8. Bake the muffins. Using a large ice cream scoop or spoon, spoon about 3 tablespoons of the batter onto the prepared pans for each top, leaving about 2 inches of room between each.
9. Bake for 10 to 14 minutes, or until a toothpick inserted into the middle comes out clean and muffins are slightly browned around edges. Cool slightly, then remove muffins from the pans and cool on a wire rack.
10. Make the drizzle. Meanwhile, in a small bowl, mix together the cream cheese, confectioners' sugar, and ¼ teaspoon of vanilla. Slowly stir in the milk, a little at a time, until well blended and a thin consistency. With a fork, drizzle over the cooled muffins.

# ORANGE GLAZED SCONES

**Prep time: 10 minutes | Cook time: 20 minutes | makes 8 scones**

**FOR THE SCONES**
Butter, for greasing the baking sheet (optional)
Flour, for the work surface
2 cups all-purpose flour
2 tablespoons granulated sugar
1 tablespoon baking powder
1 teaspoon table salt
1 teaspoon freshly grated orange zest
5 tablespoons cold unsalted butter, cut into cubes
¾ cup dried cherries, chopped
1 cup plus 2 tablespoons heavy whipping cream, divided

**FOR THE GLAZE**
½ cup confectioners' sugar
2 tablespoons freshly squeezed orange juice
**TOOLS/EQUIPMENT:**
Baking sheet
Parchment paper (optional)
Large bowl
Zester
Pastry cutter (or fork or two knives; see Cutting in Butter)
Pastry brush
Small bowl
Whisk (or fork)

1. Preheat the oven to 400°F. Grease a baking sheet or line with parchment paper.
2. Mix the dry ingredients. In a large bowl, mix together the flour, granulated sugar, baking powder, salt, and orange zest.
3. Cut in the butter.
4. Using a pastry cutter, cut in the butter until the flour mixture is coarse pea-size crumbs. Stir in the dried cherries.
5. Combine the ingredients.
6. Make a well in the center of the dry ingredients. Pour 1 cup of cream into the middle and stir until just combined.

7. Form the scones. Divide the dough in half. Place each half on a lightly floured surface and form each half into a circle about 1¼ inch thick. Cut each circle in half, and then in half again, forming 8 triangles between the two rounds.
8. Bake the scones. Place the scones on the prepared baking sheet. Brush the tops of the scones with the remaining 2 tablespoons of cream. Bake for 15 to 20 minutes or until golden brown around the edges. Cool slightly.
9. Make the glaze.
10. In a small bowl, whisk together the confectioners' sugar and orange juice until thin and smooth. Brush over the scones

# WHITE CHOCOLATE MUFFINS

**Prep time: 10 minutes | Cook time: 12 minutes | makes 24 muffins**

Butter, for greasing the pan (optional)
Flour, for dusting the pan (optional)
1¼ cups all-purpose flour
½ cup brown sugar
½ cup unsweetened cocoa powder
½ teaspoon table salt
½ teaspoon baking powder
½ teaspoon baking soda
¾ cup milk (2 percent or

whole)
⅓ cup vegetable or canola oil
2 large eggs, at room temperature
2 teaspoons vanilla extract
¼ cup finely chopped semisweet chocolate
¼ cup finely chopped white chocolate
**TOOLS/EQUIPMENT:**
Mini muffin pan
Paper liners (optional)
2 medium bowls
Wire rack

1. Preheat the oven to 375°F (190°C).
2. Grease and lightly flour a 24-cup mini muffin pan or line with paper liners.
3. Mix the dry ingredients.
4. In a medium bowl, stir together the flour, brown sugar, cocoa powder, salt, baking powder, and baking soda.
5. Mix the wet ingredients.
6. In another bowl, stir together the milk, oil, eggs, and vanilla until well blended.

7. Blend the ingredients. Make a well in the middle of the dry ingredients, then pour the wet ingredients in the middle and stir to mix. When almost blended, add the semisweet and white chocolate, and mix until just combined. Some small lumps are okay.
8. Bake the muffins. Spoon the batter into the muffin cups about ⅔ full. Bake for 8 to 12 minutes, or until a toothpick inserted into the middle of a muffin comes out clean. Cool slightly, then transfer the muffins to a wire rack to cool.

# CHEESE AND GARLIC TOPPED BREAD

Prep time: 10 minutes | Cook time: 20 minutes | serves 12

FOR THE BREAD
1 cup warm water (115°F/46°C)
2 tablespoons granulated sugar
1 (¼-ounce/7 g) envelope active dry yeast
3½ to 4 cups all-purpose flour
¼ cup plus 2 to 3 tablespoons olive oil, divided
1 teaspoon table salt
FOR THE TOPPING
2 tablespoons olive oil
½ small red onion, very thinly sliced
¼ cup shredded Parmesan cheese
2 garlic cloves, minced
½ teaspoon table salt
⅛ teaspoon freshly ground black pepper
2 tablespoons fresh rosemary
TOOLS/EQUIPMENT:
Stand mixer or large bowl
Large bowl
Plastic wrap
Baking sheet
Pastry brush

1. Prepare the yeast. In the bowl of a stand mixer with the hook attachment on, stir together the warm water, sugar, and yeast, then let it sit for about 5 minutes.
2. Combine the ingredients. Add 3 cups of flour, ¼ cup of olive oil, and 1 teaspoon of salt to the bowl. Mix on low with the hook attachment until well blended.
3. Add more flour as needed, a little at a time, until a dough forms. Raise the speed to medium, and continue kneading for 4 to 6 minutes or until the dough is smooth and elastic.
4. Let the dough rise. Grease a large bowl with 1 tablespoon of olive oil. Add the dough, turn to coat, cover with plastic wrap and place in a warm, dark, draft-free place to double in size, about 1 hour.
5. Prepare the baking sheet. Generously grease the baking sheet with 1 or 2 tablespoons of olive oil.
6. Form the bread. Transfer the dough to the prepared baking sheet. Spread the dough out into a long oblong shape, about ½ inch thick. Cover loosely with plastic wrap and return to a warm, dark, draft-free place for 15 to 20 minutes to rest and rise slightly.
7. Preheat the oven to 400°F (204°C). But first, place the oven rack at the lowest level.
8. Top the bread. Remove the plastic wrap from the dough, and using your fingertips; gently push down on the dough to leave slight dimples. Brush 2 tablespoons of olive oil over the top of the dough. Lay the onion slices on top. Sprinkle the cheese, garlic, ½ teaspoon of salt, black pepper, and rosemary on top.

# PEANUT BUTTER FROSTED CHOCO CAKE

Prep time: 15 minutes | Cook time: 35 minutes | serves 16

FOR THE CAKE:
Butter, for greasing the pans
Flour, for dusting the pans
2 cups all-purpose flour
¾ cup unsweetened cocoa powder
1 teaspoon baking soda
¾ teaspoon baking powder
½ teaspoon table salt
¾ cup (1½ sticks) unsalted butter, at room temperature
2 cups granulated sugar
3 large eggs, at room temperature
2 teaspoons vanilla extract
1½ cups milk (2 percent or whole)
1 cup mini chocolate chips
FOR THE FROSTING:
1 cup (2 sticks) unsalted butter, at room temperature
1¼ cups creamy peanut butter
3 cups confectioners' sugar
2 tablespoons milk (2 percent or whole)
TOOLS/EQUIPMENT:
2 (9-inch) round cake pans
Medium bowl
Large bowl
Electric hand mixer or stand mixer
Wire rack
Offset spatula or butter knife

1. Preheat the oven to 350°F (177°C). Grease and lightly flour 2 (9-inch) round cake pans. Mix the dry ingredients. In a medium bowl, stir together the flour, cocoa powder, baking soda, baking powder, and salt.
2. Cream the butter and sugar. In a large bowl, beat ¾ cup of butter with an electric mixer on medium speed for about 10 seconds, or until smooth. Beat in the granulated sugar until well blended and light and fluffy, about 2 minutes. Beat in the eggs, one at a time, beating after each egg is added. Beat in the vanilla.
3. Combine the ingredients. Alternate adding the flour mixture and 1½ cups of milk to the butter mixture, beating on low after each addition until batter is just combined. Fold in the chocolate chips.
4. Bake the cake. Spoon the batter evenly among the 2 prepared cake pans. Bake for 30 to 35 minutes, or until a toothpick inserted into the center comes out clean. Cool slightly, then remove the cakes from the pans to finish cooling on a wire rack.
5. Make the frosting. In a large bowl, blend 1 cup of butter and the peanut butter with an electric mixer on low speed. Beat in the confectioners' sugar. Slowly add 1 to 2 tablespoons of milk, beating until the frosting is a spreading consistency.
6. Frost the cake. When the cakes are completely cool, place one layer, flat side up, on a serving plate. Spread the frosting over the top with an offset spatula or butter knife. Place the second cake layer on top, flat side down. Spread more frosting on the top and sides of cake as desired.

# SWEET BREAD ROLLS

**Prep time: 10 minutes | Cook time: 25 minutes | makes 12 bagels**

FOR THE BAGELS
1 cup warm water (115°F/46°C)
1 tablespoon granulated sugar
1 (¼-ounce) envelope active dry yeast
2½ to 3 cups all-purpose flour
1 teaspoon table salt
1 teaspoon olive oil, plus 1 to 2 tablespoons olive oil, divided
FOR THE WATER BATH
8 cups water

1 tablespoon granulated sugar
FOR THE TOPPING
½ cup shredded Parmesan or Asiago cheese
TOOLS/EQUIPMENT:
Stand mixer (optional) or large bowl
Large bowl
2 baking sheets
Large saucepan
Slotted spoon

1. Prepare the yeast. In the bowl of a stand mixer with the hook attachment on, stir together the 1 cup of water, 1 tablespoon of sugar, and the yeast, then let it sit for about 5 minutes.

2. Make the dough. Add 2 cups of flour and the salt to the bowl. Mix on low with the hook attachment until well combined, adding more flour, a little at a time, until a dough forms. Increase the speed to medium, and continue kneading for 4 to 6 minutes or until the dough is smooth and elastic.

3. Let it rise. Grease a large bowl with oil. Add the dough, turn it to coat, then cover with plastic wrap and place in a warm, dark, draft-free place to double in size, about 1 hour.

4. Prepare the baking sheet. Generously grease the baking sheet with 1 or 2 tablespoons of olive oil, or line with parchment paper.

5. Form the bagels. When the dough has doubled, punch it down. Divide the dough into 12 balls. Roll each ball into a log 5 to 6 inches long. Join the ends together, place fingers through the hole and roll the ends together until smooth. Place the bagels on the prepared baking sheet. Cover the bagels with a clean, light towel, and place in a warm, dark, draft-free place for about 30 minutes or until dough has risen a bit more.

6. Preheat the oven to 400°F. Grease another baking sheet or line with parchment paper.

7. Prepare the water bath. In a large saucepan over high heat, add the 8 cups of water and 1 tablespoon sugar. Bring to a boil, stirring to combine.

8. Dip the bagels in the water bath. In batches, add a few bagels at a time to the boiling water for 20 seconds, then with a slotted spoon, turn the bagels over and cook an additional 20 seconds. Remove the bagels from the water, gently shaking off excess water, and place on the prepared baking sheet.

9. Bake the bagels. Bake for 15 to 25 minutes or until golden brown. In the last 5 minutes of baking, sprinkle the bagels with the cheese and continue baking.

9. Bake the bread. Bake on the lowest oven rack for 15 to 20 minutes, or until golden brown.

# BROWN BUTTER COOKIES

**Prep time: 10 minutes | Cook time: 12 minutes | makes 18 biscuits**

2 cups all-purpose flour
2 teaspoons baking powder
½ teaspoon table salt
½ cup (1 stick) cold unsalted butter, cut into small cubes
¾ cup cold milk (2 percent or whole)
TOOLS/EQUIPMENT:
Medium bowl
Pastry cutter
2 baking sheets
Parchment paper (optional)

1. Preheat the oven to 425°F (218°C). Mix the dry ingredients.

2. In a medium bowl, mix together the flour, baking powder, and salt until blended. Cut in the butter.

3. Using a pastry cutter or the back of a fork, cut the butter into the flour mixture until the mixture is even and crumbly. Add the wet ingredients.

4. Mix the milk into the flour mixture, and stir until the dough is just combined (don't overmix) and a soft moist dough forms.

5. Bake the biscuits. Using a spoon, drop the biscuit dough onto 2 nonstick baking sheets or baking sheets lined with parchment paper to make 18 biscuits. Bake for 9 to 12 minutes, or until browned on the bottom.

# BUTTER TOPPED SANDWICH BREAD

**Prep time: 10 minutes | Cook time: 40 minutes | serves 24**

FOR THE BREAD
2 cups warm milk (2 percent or whole, 105-115°F/46°C)
2 tablespoons granulated sugar
1 (¼-ounce/7 g) envelope active dry yeast
2 tablespoons butter, at room temperature
5 to 6 cups all-purpose flour
2 teaspoons table salt
1 tablespoon vegetable or canola oil
Butter, for greasing the pans
FOR THE TOPPING
2 tablespoons butter, melted
TOOLS/EQUIPMENT:
Stand mixer or large bowl
Large bowl
Plastic wrap
2 loaf pans (8½ by 4½ by 2½ inches)
Pastry brush
Wire rack

1. Prepare the yeast. In the bowl of a stand mixer with the hook attachment on, stir together the warm milk, sugar, and yeast, then let it sit for about 5 minutes.

2. Combine the ingredients. Add the 2 tablespoons room-temperature butter, 4 cups of flour, and salt to the yeast mixture. Mix on low with the hook attachment until well blended.

3. Add more flour as needed, a little at a time, until a dough forms. Raise the speed to medium, and continue kneading for 4 to 6 minutes, or until the dough is smooth and elastic.

4. Let it rise. Grease a large bowl with oil. Add the dough, turn it to coat, cover with plastic wrap and place in a warm, dark, draft-free place to double in size, about 1 hour.

5. Punch down the dough, form it into 2 loaves, and place each in a greased loaf pan. Lightly brush the tops of the loaves with the melted butter. Cover with plastic wrap, and place in a warm, dark, draft-free place to rise again, about 30 minutes.

6. Preheat the oven to 350°F.Bake the bread

7. Bake for 30 to 40 minutes or until browned and hollow-sounding when lightly tapped. Cool slightly, then remove and place on a wire rack to finish cooling.

# HONEYED MILKY BREAD

**Prep time: 20 minutes | Cook time: 55 minutes | serves 24**

1 (¼-ounce) envelope active dry yeast
¼ cup warm water (105 to 115°F/46°C)
2 cups milk (2 percent or whole)
4 tablespoons unsalted butter, divided
2 tablespoons honey
1 teaspoon table salt
1¼ cups old-fashioned rolled oats
4 to 5 cups all-purpose flour, plus more to flour the work surface
Butter, for greasing the pans
TOOLS/EQUIPMENT:
Large bowl
Small saucepan
Whisk or spoon
2 loaf pans (approximately 8½ by 4½ by 2½ inches)
Aluminum foil
Pastry brush
Wire rack

1. Prepare the yeast. In a large bowl, stir together the yeast and warm water. Let sit for about 5 minutes.

2. Heat the milk. In a small saucepan over medium heat, add the milk, 3 tablespoons of butter, the honey, and salt. Whisk until the butter has melted and the mixture is blended. Let this mixture cool a bit, then pour into the yeast mixture.

3. Blend the ingredients. Add the oats and 4 cups of flour to the yeast mixture, and stir until well blended. Add more flour as needed until a sticky dough forms.

4. Knead the dough. Place the dough on a well-floured surface. Knead the dough 6 to 8 minutes, adding flour as necessary, until smooth and elastic.

5. Let it rise. Divide the dough in half, form into two loaves, and place each in a well-greased loaf pan. Cover lightly with plastic wrap and place in a dark, warm, draft-free place to double in size, about 1 hour.

6. Preheat the oven to 350°F (177°C).

7. Bake the bread. Bake the bread for about 25 minutes, then cover with aluminum foil to prevent further browning. Continue baking for an additional 20 to 30 minutes or until the loaves sound hollow when lightly tapped.

8. Melt the remaining tablespoon of butter and brush it on the tops of the loaves. Cool slightly, then transfer to a wire rack to finish cooling.

# BUTTER FROSTED VANILLA CAKE

**Prep time: 10 minutes | Cook time: 25 minutes | makes 24 cake pops**

**FOR THE CAKE**
Butter, for greasing the pan
Flour, for dusting the pan
1 cup all-purpose flour
1 teaspoon baking powder
¼ teaspoon baking soda
¼ teaspoon table salt
⅓ cup unsalted butter, at room temperature
⅔ cup granulated sugar
2 large eggs, at room temperature
1½ teaspoons vanilla extract
⅓ cup milk (2 percent or whole)
**FOR THE FROSTING**
4 tablespoons unsalted butter, at room temperature
2 cups confectioners' sugar
2 to 4 tablespoons milk (2 percent or whole)
**FOR THE CANDY COATING**
White candy melts, about 2 (10-ounce/283 g) bags
Sprinkles
**TOOLS/EQUIPMENT:**
9-inch round cake pan
Medium bowl
Large bowl
Electric stand or hand mixer
Wire rack
Baking sheet
Wax or parchment paper
Double boiler (or see Make Your Own Double Boiler)
Spatula
White lollipop sticks
Cake pop stand, box, or foam

1   Preheat the oven to 350°F (177°C) . Grease and lightly flour a 9-inch round cake pan. Mix the dry ingredients. In a medium bowl, stir together the flour, baking powder, baking soda, and salt.

2   Cream the butter and sugar. In a large bowl, beat ⅓ cup of room-temperature butter with an electric mixer on medium speed for about 10 seconds or until smooth.

3   Beat in the granulated sugar until well combined and light and fluffy, about 2 minutes. Beat in the eggs, one at a time, beating after each egg is added. Beat in the vanilla.

4   Combine the ingredients. Alternate adding some of the flour mixture and ⅓ cup of milk to the butter mixture, beating on low after each addition, until the batter is just combined.

5   Bake the cake. Pour the cake batter into the prepared pan. Bake for 20 to 25 minutes, or until a toothpick inserted into the middle comes out clean. Cool slightly, and then remove the cake from the pan to finish cooling on a wire rack.

6   Make the frosting. When the cake is completely cooled, prepare the frosting. In a medium bowl, add 4 tablespoons of room-temperature butter and beat with an electric mixer for about 10 seconds, or until smooth. Gradually beat in the confectioners' sugar. Add 2 tablespoons of milk and beat until smooth, adding a little more milk at a time as needed. The frosting should be a little on the thicker side.

7   Stir together the cake and frosting. In a large bowl, crumble the cooled cake into pieces. Add ¼ cup of frosting. Using a sturdy spatula or large spoon, mix together the cake and frosting.

8   Add a little more frosting at a time until the cake is fully crumbled and the mixture starts to clump together.

9   Form the cake balls. Scoop the cake mixture out into 1-inch balls, roll in your hands if necessary to form a ball, and place on a baking sheet lined with wax or parchment paper. Refrigerate for about 1 hour, or until the cake balls are firm.

10  Dip the cake balls. Place the candy melts in the top of a double boiler. Place over boiling water, and then reduce the heat to low.

11  Stir constantly, until the candy melts are melted and smooth. Dip about ¼ inch of the tip of a lollipop stick into the melted candy melt, then insert the stick into the cake ball.

12  Dip the cake balls, one at a time, in the candy melts, covering the entire cake ball and just below to the stick. You can pour the melted candy melts into a tall narrow container or glass for easier dipping. Before the candy melt hardens, sprinkle the sprinkles on top of the cake balls.

13  Place the cake pops on a cake pop stand or in foam (see Pro Tip) to stand upright. Repeat with the remaining cake balls.

# ORANGE BUTTER CAKE

**Prep time: 15 minutes | Cook time: 90 minutes | serves 16**

FOR THE CAKE
Butter, for greasing the pan
Flour, for dusting the pan
3 cups all-purpose flour
½ teaspoon baking powder
½ teaspoon table salt
1½ cups (3 sticks) unsalted
butter, at room temperature
3 cups granulated sugar
5 large eggs, at room temperature
2 tablespoons freshly grated
orange zest
2 teaspoons vanilla extract
1 cup milk (2 percent or whole)
FOR THE ORANGE GLAZE
½ cup granulated sugar
½ cup freshly squeezed orange
juice (from 2 or 3 oranges)
TOOLS/EQUIPMENT:
1 (10-inch) tube pan
Large bowl
Electric hand mixer or stand
mixer
Zester
Small saucepan
Pastry brush

1   Preheat the oven to 350°F (177°C). Grease and flour a 10-inch tube pan.

2   Combine the dry ingredients. In a large bowl, combine the flour, baking powder, and salt until well combined.

3   Cream the butter and sugar. In a separate large bowl, beat the butter with an electric mixer on medium speed until smooth, about 10 seconds. Beat in 3 cups of sugar until well blended and light and fluffy, about 2 minutes. Beat in the eggs, one at a time, then beat in the orange zest and vanilla until blended.

4   Combine the ingredients. Alternate beating in the dry ingredients and the milk into the butter mixture until just combined.

5   Bake the cake. Pour the batter into the tube pan. Bake for 60 to 90 minutes, or until a toothpick inserted into the middle comes out clean.

6   Prepare the glaze. In a small saucepan over medium heat, heat ½ cup of sugar and orange juice, stirring until slightly thickened, about 5 minutes. Brush the glaze over the top and sides of the warm cake.

# WALNUT FILLED CINNAMON CAKE

**Prep time: 10 minutes | Cook time: 60 minutes | serves 16**

FOR THE FILLING
½ cup granulated sugar
1 cup chopped walnuts or pecans
1½ teaspoons cinnamon
FOR THE CAKE
2¼ cups all-purpose flour
2 teaspoons baking powder
½ teaspoon baking soda
¼ teaspoon table salt
⅓ cup unsalted butter, at room
temperature
1 cup granulated sugar
⅓ cup vegetable or canola oil
2 large eggs, at room temperature
2 teaspoons vanilla extract
TOOLS/EQUIPMENT:
10-inch tube pan (with
removable bottom)
Small bowl
2 large bowls
Electric hand mixer or stand
mixer
Wire rack
Butter, for greasing the pan
Flour, for dusting the pan
1 cup sour cream or plain Greek
yogurt

1   Preheat the oven to 350°F. Grease and flour a 10-inch tube pan. Make the filling. In a small bowl, mix together ½ cup of sugar, the walnuts or pecans, and cinnamon until well combined.

2   Blend the dry ingredients. In a large bowl, mix the flour, baking powder, baking soda, and salt until well blended.

3   Cream the butter and sugar.

4   In a separate large bowl, beat the butter with an electric mixer on medium speed for about 10 seconds, or until smooth. Beat in 1 cup of sugar and the oil, until well blended and light and fluffy, about 2 minutes. Beat in the eggs, one at a time, beating after each egg is added. Beat in the vanilla, and then beat in the sour cream.

5   Combine the ingredients. Slowly beat the butter mixture into the dry ingredients until just blended.

6   Assemble the cake. Spoon half of the cake batter into the tube pan. Spread with a spoon to form an even layer across the bottom of the pan. Sprinkle half of the nut filling over the batter, then top with the remaining batter.

7   Bake the cake. Bake for 45 to 60 minutes, or until a toothpick inserted into the middle comes out clean. Cool slightly, and then remove from the pan to cool completely on a wire rack.

# HOMEMADE SWEET CREAM CAKE

Prep time: 10 minutes | Cook time: 45 minutes | serves 12

1½ cups confectioners' sugar, sifted
1 cup all-purpose flour, sifted
1½ cups egg whites (from 10 to 12 large eggs)
1½ teaspoons cream of tartar
1 teaspoon vanilla extract
1 cup granulated sugar
TOOLS/EQUIPMENT:

Medium bowl
Large bowl
Stand mixer with whisk attachment or electric hand mixer
Sifter (or mesh strainer)
10-inch tube pan (with removable bottom)
Wire rack or sturdy glass bottle

1  Preheat the oven to 350°F. But first, make sure the oven rack is in the lowest position.

2  Combine the sugar and flour. In a medium bowl, mix together the confectioners' sugar and flour until well blended with no lumps.

3  Whip up the egg whites. In a large bowl, add the egg whites (see Separating Eggs), cream of tartar, and vanilla.

4  Beat on medium until the whites start getting foamy, 1 to 2 minutes. Increase the speed to medium-high, and continue beating until the egg whites become thick and opaque, 1 to 2 minutes.

5  Add the granulated sugar. With the mixer on medium-high speed, slowly add the granulated sugar, 1 to 2 tablespoons at a time. Continue beating until the egg whites are shiny and stiff peaks form, 4 to 6 minutes.

6  Fold in the dry ingredients. Gently sift about a quarter of the flour and confectioners' sugar mixture over the egg whites. Very gently fold in the flour mixture with a large rubber spatula, being careful to not deflate the egg whites. Repeat with the remaining flour and confectioners' sugar until just folded in.

7  Bake the cake. Pour the batter into an ungreased 10-inch tube pan. Lightly run a butter knife through the batter to remove any air bubbles.

8  Bake for 35 to 45 minutes, or until the top is lightly browned and springs back when lightly touched. Set the cake upside down over a wire rack or sturdy glass bottle to cool. When cooled, run a butter knife around the edge to loosen before inverting onto a plate.

# CITRUSY VANILLA CAKE

Prep time: 15 minutes | Cook time: 60 minutes | serves 12

FOR THE CAKE
Butter, for greasing the pan
Flour, for dusting the pan
⅓ cup milk (2 percent or whole)
2 tablespoons freshly squeezed lemon juice
1½ cups all-purpose flour
¼ teaspoon baking powder
¼ teaspoon baking soda
¼ teaspoon table salt
½ cup (1 stick) unsalted butter, at room temperature
1 cup granulated sugar
2 large eggs, at room temperature
½ teaspoon vanilla extract
1 tablespoon freshly grated

lemon zest
FOR THE GLAZE
¾ cup confectioners' sugar
2 teaspoons freshly squeezed lemon juice
3 tablespoons milk (2 percent or whole)
TOOLS/EQUIPMENT:
Loaf pan (approximately 8½ by 4½ by 2½ inches)
Small bowl
Medium bowl
Large bowl
Electric hand mixer or stand mixer
Zester
Wire rack
Whisk (or fork)

1  Preheat the oven to 350°F. Grease and lightly flour a loaf pan. Make the sour milk.

2  In a small bowl, add ⅓ cup of milk and 2 tablespoons of lemon juice, and stir to combine. Let sit about 10 minutes.

3  Mix the dry ingredients. In a medium bowl, stir together the flour, baking powder, baking soda, and salt.

4  Cream the butter and sugar. In a large bowl, beat the butter with an electric mixer on medium speed for about 10 seconds, or until smooth.

5  Beat in the granulated sugar until well blended and light and fluffy, about 2 minutes. Beat in the eggs, one at a time, beating after each egg is added. Beat in the vanilla and lemon zest.

6  Combine all ingredients. Alternate adding the flour mixture and the milk mixture to the butter mixture, beating on low after each addition, until the batter is just combined.

7  Bake the cake. Pour the cake batter into the prepared pan. Bake for 45 to 60 minutes, or until a toothpick inserted into the middle comes out clean. Cool slightly, and then remove the cake from the pan to finish cooling on a wire rack.

8  Make the glaze. In a medium bowl, whisk together the confectioners' sugar, 2 teaspoons of lemon juice, and 1 tablespoon of milk. Whisk in more milk as needed until thick but spreadable. Spoon the glaze over the top of the cake, so it can drizzle down the sides.

# GOLDEN BUTTER CHIVE COOKIES

**Prep time: 10 minutes | Cook time: 17 minutes | makes 16 biscuits**

Butter, for greasing the pan
2¾ cups plus 2 tablespoons all-purpose flour
4½ teaspoons baking powder
1 teaspoon table salt
6 tablespoons cold, cubed unsalted butter
½ cup chopped fresh chives
1 to 1½ cups cold buttermilk
Flour, for the work surface
3 tablespoons melted unsalted butter
TOOLS/EQUIPMENT:
Cast-iron pan or skillet (about 10½-inch diameter)
Large bowl
Pastry cutter
2-inch round cookie or biscuit cutter
Pastry brush)

1. Preheat the oven to 425°F (218°C). Set the oven rack at the lowest level. Grease a cast-iron pan.
2. Mix the dry ingredients. In a large bowl, mix together the flour, baking powder, and salt until combined.
3. Cut in the butter. With a pastry cutter or back of a fork, cut in the 6 tablespoons of cold butter, until the mixture resembles coarse crumbs. Stir in the chives.
4. Add the wet ingredients.
5. Add 1 cup buttermilk to the flour mixture. Stir to combine, and add more milk as necessary until the dough just comes together but is still moist. Be careful not to overwork the dough or the biscuits may come out dry.
6. Form the biscuits. Place the dough on a floured surface. Gently press the dough until 1 inch thick. With a 2-inch round cutter, cut the dough into 16 biscuits.
7. Bake the biscuits. Place the biscuits next to each other in the prepared pan. Bake on the bottom rack for 12 to 17 minutes or until golden brown. Brush with the 3 tablespoons of melted butter. Cool slightly before serving.

# HONEYED ALMOND CHOCO CAKE

**Prep time: 10 minutes | Cook time: 30 minutes | serves 4**

Butter, for greasing the ramekins
6 tablespoons unsalted butter
¼ cup honey
⅔ cup dark chocolate chips
1 cup finely ground almonds (or almond flour)
2 large eggs, at room temperature, beaten
1 teaspoon vanilla extract
½ teaspoon table salt
TOOLS/EQUIPMENT:
4 (4-ounce/113 g) ramekins
Baking sheet
Double boiler
Medium bowl
Whisk or fork

1. Preheat the oven to 350°F. Lightly grease 4 small ramekins and place them on a baking sheet. Melt the chocolate.
2. Add the butter, honey, and chocolate chips to the top of a double boiler over boiling water, then reduce the heat to low, mixing until smooth. Set aside to cool completely, about 30 to 45 minutes.
3. Whisk the ingredients. In a medium bowl, whisk together the almonds, eggs, vanilla, and salt until well blended. Slowly whisk in the cooled chocolate mixture.
4. Bake the cakes. Bake for 20 to 30 minutes, or until a toothpick inserted into the middle comes out clean.

# CHOCOLATE TOPPED ICE CREAM CAKE

Prep time: 30 minutes | Cook time: 25 minutes | serves 16

FOR THE CAKE
Butter, for greasing the pans
Flour, for dusting the pans
1½ cups all-purpose flour
½ cup unsweetened cocoa powder
1 teaspoon baking powder
¼ teaspoon baking soda
¾ cup granulated sugar
½ cup brown sugar
¾ cup (1½ sticks) unsalted butter, melted and cooled
2 large eggs, at room temperature
1 teaspoon vanilla extract

1 cup milk (2 percent or whole)
4 cups ice cream, any flavor
FOR THE CHOCOLATE TOPPING
1 cup semisweet chocolate chips
2 teaspoons corn syrup
½ cup heavy whipping cream
TOOLS/EQUIPMENT:
2 (9-inch) cake pans
Medium bowl
Large bowl
Wire rack
Small saucepan

1. Preheat the oven to 350°F (177°C). Grease and lightly flour 2 (9-inch) round cake pans.

2. Blend the flour mixture. In a medium bowl, mix together the flour, cocoa powder, baking powder, and baking soda until well blended.

3. Blend the sugar and butter. In a large bowl, mix the granulated sugar, brown sugar, and butter until well blended, about 2 minutes. Add the eggs one at time, beating after each addition, then beat in the vanilla. Combine the ingredients.

4. Alternate beating in the dry ingredients and the milk to the wet ingredients until just combined. Bake the cakes. Pour the batter evenly into the 2 prepared pans. Bake for 20 to 25 minutes, or until a toothpick inserted into the middle comes out clean. Cool slightly, then remove from pans and place on a wire rack to cool completely.

5. Assemble the cake. Let the ice cream sit on the counter for 5 to 10 minutes, until soft but not soupy.

6. Place the bottom cake layer, flat side up, on a serving plate. Spoon the ice cream on top of the bottom cake layer, and spread the ice cream to the edge of the cake with a spoon. Top with the other cake layer, flat side down, and press gently on the cake to help spread the ice cream to the edges. Place the cake in the freezer for 1 to 2 hours, or until firm.

7. Prepare the topping. In a medium bowl, add the chocolate chips and corn syrup. In a small saucepan over low heat, heat the heavy cream, whisking continuously, until it just starts to boil. Pour the hot cream over the chocolate chips. Let sit about 1 minute, then stir to combine until smooth. Let cool.

8. Top the cake. Spoon the cooled chocolate over the top of the cake and let it drip down the sides of the cake. Return the cake to the freezer until ready to serve, at least a half hour. Let the cake sit at room temperature for 10 to 20 minutes to soften before slicing and serving.

# BANANA BUTTER BREAD

Prep time: 20 minutes | Cook time: 60 minutes | serves 12

Butter, for greasing the pan
Flour, for dusting the pan
1⅔ cups all-purpose flour
1 teaspoon baking soda
½ teaspoon cinnamon
½ teaspoon table salt
2 large eggs, at room temperature
¾ cup granulated sugar

1½ cups mashed, very ripe bananas (3 to 5 bananas)
½ cup vegetable or canola oil
2 tablespoons plain Greek yogurt
1 teaspoon vanilla extract
TOOLS/EQUIPMENT:
Loaf pan (8½ by 4½ by 2½ inches)
2 medium bowls

1 Preheat the oven to 350°F (177°C). Lightly grease and flour a loaf pan.

2 Mix the dry ingredients. In a medium bowl, mix together the flour, baking soda, cinnamon, and salt until well combined.

3 Mix remaining ingredients. In another medium bowl, beat together the eggs and sugar for 3 to 5 minutes, or until light and fluffy. Stir in the banana, oil, yogurt, and vanilla until just combined.

4 Combine the ingredients. Make a well in the center of the dry ingredients. Pour the wet ingredients into the well. Stir until just combined.

5 Bake the bread. Pour the batter into the prepared loaf pan. Bake at 350°F (177°C) for 45 to 60 minutes, or until a toothpick inserted in the center comes out clean.

# CHAPTER 9: FEEL COOL FRESH DRINKS

# HOMEMADE ICE CREAM SHAKE

Prep time: 15 minutes | Cook time: 0 minutes | serves 4

4 cups vanilla ice cream
½ cup milk
Pinch salt
**COOKING EQUIPMENT**

2 to 4 glasses
Food processor
Rubber spatula

1. Place glasses in freezer and chill until ready to serve. Remove ice cream from freezer and let sit at room temperature to soften, about 15 minutes.
2. Add softened ice cream, milk, and salt to food processor. Lock lid into place. Turn on processor and process for 30 seconds. Stop processor. Remove lid

and use rubber spatula to scrape down sides of bowl.
3. Lock lid back into place. Turn on processor and process until smooth, about 30 seconds. Stop processor. Carefully remove processor blade (ask an adult for help).
4. Pour milkshakes into chilled glasses and serve immediately

# POMEGRANATE SYRUP

Prep time: 15 minutes | Cook time: 45 minutes | makes 1 cup

8 allspice berries
¾ cup sugar
⅔ cup unsweetened 100 percent pomegranate juice
**COOKING EQUIPMENT**
Zipper-lock plastic bag

Small saucepan
Whisk
Fine-mesh strainer
Medium bowl
Jar with tight-fitting lid

1. Place allspice berries in zipper-lock plastic bag. Seal bag, making sure to press out all air. Use small saucepan to lightly crush berries.
2. In small saucepan, combine sugar, pomegranate juice, and crushed allspice berries. Heat mixture over medium heat, whisking occasionally, until sugar has dissolved, about 5 minutes. Do not let it boil.
3. Turn off heat. Slide saucepan to cool burner. Let

mixture cool completely, about 30 minutes.
4. Place fine-mesh strainer over medium bowl. Pour cooled mixture through strainer into bowl and discard allspice berries.
5. Pour strained grenadine into jar with tight-fitting lid. (Grenadine can be refrigerated for up to 1 month.)

# WATERMELON CITRUS SOFT DRINK

Prep time: 15 minutes | Cook time: 20 minutes | serves 6

8 cups (1-inch pieces) seedless watermelon (2½ pounds)
2 cups water
¼ cup lime juice, squeezed from 2 limes, plus lime wedges for serving
2 tablespoons honey
⅛ teaspoon salt
Ice

Fresh mint leaves (optional)
**COOKING EQUIPMENT**
Fine-mesh strainer
Pitcher
Blender
Dish towel
Rubber spatula
Glasses

1. Place fine-mesh strainer over pitcher; set aside.
2. Add half of chopped watermelon and half of water to blender jar. Place lid on top of blender and hold firmly in place with folded dish towel (see this page). Turn on blender and process until smooth, about 30 seconds.
3. Stop blender and remove lid. Pour mixture into fine-mesh strainer set over pitcher. Use rubber spatula to stir and press on watermelon bits to get out as much

juice as possible. Discard solids in strainer.
4. Repeat blending and straining in steps 2 and 3 with second half of watermelon and water.
5. Add lime juice, honey, and salt to pitcher. Use rubber spatula to stir until well combined.
6. To serve, place ice in glasses and pour agua fresca over ice. Add lime wedge and mint (if using) to each glass. (Agua fresca can be refrigerated for up to 5 days; stir to recombine before serving.)

# FROZEN CITRUS DRINK

**Prep time: 15 minutes | Cook time: 30 minutes | serves 4**

7 limes
1 cup sugar
4½ cups cold water
COOKING EQUIPMENT
Cutting board
Chef's knife
Large bowl
Potato masher
Citrus juicer
Rubber spatula
Fine-mesh strainer
Large pitcher
2 ice cube trays
Blender
Dish towel
Glasses

1.   Cut 1 lime in half through both ends. Lay lime halves, flat side down, on cutting board, then cut each half crosswise into thin semicircles (see photo, right).

2.   Add lime slices and sugar to large bowl. Use potato masher to mash sugar and lime slices together until sugar is completely wet, about 1 minute. Set aside.

3.   Cut remaining 6 limes in half crosswise. Use citrus juicer to squeeze lime juice into bowl with sugar and lime slices.

4.   Pour water into bowl and use rubber spatula to stir mixture until sugar is completely dissolved, about 1 minute.

5.   Set fine-mesh strainer over large pitcher. Carefully pour mixture through strainer into bowl. Use rubber spatula to stir and press on limes to get out as much juice as possible. Discard lime slices in strainer.

6.   Carefully pour half of lime mixture into 2 ice cube trays. Place trays in freezer and freeze until frozen solid, 2 to 3 hours. Place remaining lime juice mixture in refrigerator.

7.   When limeade cubes are frozen, pop them out of ice cube trays and add to blender jar. Pour remaining lime juice mixture over top.

8.   Place lid on top of blender and hold firmly in place with folded dish towel (see this page). Turn on blender and process until smooth, 30 to 60 seconds. Stop blender. Pour into glasses and serve immediately.

# CINNAMON ALMOND MILK DRINK

**Prep time: 15 minutes | Cook time: 0 minutes | serves 4**

4½ cups water
1¼ cups whole blanched almonds
½ cup sugar
⅓ cup long-grain white rice
1½ teaspoons vanilla extract
1 teaspoon ground cinnamon
¼ teaspoon salt
1 cup evaporated milk
Ice
COOKING EQUIPMENT
2 large bowls
Plastic wrap
Fine-mesh strainer
Cheesecloth
Blender
Dish towel
Pitcher
Rubber spatula
Glasses

1.   In large bowl, combine water, almonds, sugar, rice, vanilla, cinnamon, and salt. Cover with plastic wrap and let sit at room temperature for at least 12 hours or up to 24 hours.

2.   When mixture is ready, set fine-mesh strainer over second large bowl. Line strainer with triple layer of cheesecloth that overhangs edges; set aside.

3.   Carefully pour almond mixture into blender jar. Place lid on top of blender and hold firmly in place with folded dish towel. Turn on blender and process until smooth, 30 to 60 seconds. Stop blender.

4.   Carefully strain blended almond mixture through cheesecloth-lined strainer into large bowl, following photos, right.

5.   Pour strained almond liquid into pitcher. Add evaporated milk to pitcher and use rubber spatula to stir until well combined.

6.   To serve, place ice in glasses. Pour horchata over ice. (Horchata can be refrigerated for up to 3 days.)

# HONEYED MANGO YOGURT DRINK

**Prep time: 15 minutes | Cook time: 0 minutes | serves 4**

4 cups frozen mango chunks,
thawed
2½ cups plain whole-milk yogurt
1 cup water
2 tablespoons honey
2 teaspoons lime juice, squeezed
from 1 lime
⅛ teaspoon salt

Ice
COOKING EQUIPMENT
Blender
Dish towel
Rubber spatula
Fine-mesh strainer
Large pitcher
Glasses

1. Add mango, yogurt, water, honey, lime juice, and salt to blender jar. Place lid on top of blender and hold firmly in place with folded dish towel (see this page). Turn on blender and process for 30 seconds. Stop blender.

2. Remove lid and scrape down sides of blender jar with rubber spatula. Replace lid, turn on blender, and process until smooth, 30 to 60 seconds. Stop blender.

3. Set fine-mesh strainer over pitcher. Carefully pour half of mango mixture into strainer. Use rubber spatula to press and stir on mango bits to get out as much liquid as possible.

4. Discard solids left in strainer. Repeat straining with remaining mango mixture. To serve, place ice in glasses. Pour mango lassi over ice.

# HONEYED BERRY YOGURT SMOOTHIE

**Prep time: 15 minutes | Cook time: 10 minutes | serves 4**

1 ripe banana, peeled and
broken into 4 pieces
1 tablespoon honey
Pinch salt
2 cups frozen mixed berries
1 cup plain yogurt

½ cup pomegranate juice
COOKING EQUIPMENT
Blender
Dish towel
Rubber spatula
Glasses

1. Place banana, honey, and salt in blender jar. Place lid on top of blender and hold firmly in place with folded dish towel (see this page). Turn on blender and process until smooth, about 30 seconds. Stop blender.

2. Remove lid. Add berries, yogurt, and pomegranate juice. Replace lid, turn on blender, and

process for 30 seconds. Stop blender and scrape down sides of blender jar with rubber spatula.

3. Replace lid, turn on blender, and continue to process until smooth, about 30 seconds longer. Pour into glasses and serve.

# FLAVORSOME SYRUP

**Prep time: 5 minutes | Cook time: 0 minutes | makes 1 cup**

⅔ cup sugar
⅔ cup water
1 flavored syrup ingredient
COOKING EQUIPMENT

Jar with tight-fitting lid
Fine-mesh strainer (for
Flavored Syrups)
Medium bowl (for Flavored
Syrups)

1. In jar, combine sugar, water, and flavored syrup ingredient (if using). Cover jar with lid to seal. Shake jar vigorously until sugar dissolves, about 2 minutes.

2. Let jar sit on counter until syrup turns clear, about 5 minutes. If making a flavored syrup, let jar sit on counter for 30 minutes to infuse flavor, and continue on to step 3.

3. If making flavored syrup, place fine-mesh strainer over bowl. Remove jar lid and pour syrup mixture through strainer into bowl. Discard solids in strainer.

4. Pour flavored syrup back into jar. (Simple syrup can be refrigerated in airtight container for up to 1 month.)

# CHAPTER 10: LIP SMACKING SWEETS

# BUTTER SAUTÉED APPLE AND WALNUTS

**Prep time: 10 minutes | Cook time: 25 minutes | serves 4**

2½ tablespoons butter
6 firm, tart apples, such as
Granny Smith or Honey crisp,
peeled and cut into small cubes
¾ cup brown sugar
½ cup chopped walnuts or
raisins (or both)
1½ teaspoons ground cinnamon

½ teaspoon ground nutmeg
Pinch salt
TOOLS/EQUIPMENT
Cutting board
Knife
Large sauté pan
Wooden spoon
Small mason jars or serving bowls

1. Cook the apples.
2. In a large sauté pan over medium-low heat, melt the butter. Add the apples and brown sugar and sauté, stirring often, for 15 minutes, or until the apples are soft (see Troubleshooting).
3. Add the extras. Add the walnuts and/or raisins, cinnamon, nutmeg, and salt. Stir to mix well, and sauté for an additional 6 to 8 minutes, or until thickened.
4. Serve. Remove from the heat, spoon into small mason jars or serving bowls, and serve.

# CITRUS RASPBERRY ICE

**Prep time: 10 minutes | Cook time: 0 minutes | makes 1 quart**

⅔ cup water
¼ cup lemon juice, squeezed
from 2 lemons
4 cups (20 ounces/ 566 g)
raspberries
1⅓ cups sugar
⅛ teaspoon salt
COOKING EQUIPMENT
4-cup liquid measuring cup

Food processor
Fine-mesh strainer
Large bowl
Ladle
2 ice cube trays
Butter knife
Rubber spatula
Quart-size storage container

1. Combine water and lemon juice in 4-cup liquid measuring cup and set aside.
2. Add raspberries, sugar, and salt to food processor. Lock lid into place. Hold down pulse button for 1 second, then release. Repeat until raspberries are broken down, about five 1-second pulses.
3. Turn on processor. With processor running, pour water mixture through feed tube. Continue to process until sugar has dissolved and mixture is smooth, about 1 minute. Stop processor. Remove lid and carefully remove processor blade.
4. Set fine-mesh strainer over large bowl. Pour raspberry mixture into fine-mesh strainer. Use ladle to stir and press mixture to push liquid through strainer into bowl. Discard solids in strainer.
5. Transfer raspberry mixture to now-empty liquid measuring cup. Pour raspberry mixture into 2 ice cube trays. Place in freezer and freeze until solid, at least 8 hours or overnight.
6. Remove ice cube trays from freezer and let sit on counter until softened slightly, 15 to 20 minutes.
7. Use butter knife to loosen cubes from ice cube trays and transfer cubes to clean processor (see photo 1, below). Lock lid into place. Hold down pulse button for 1 second, then release. Repeat until cubes begin to break down, about 10 pulses.
8. Turn on processor and process until cubes are mostly broken down, about 30 seconds. Stop processor. Remove lid and use rubber spatula to scrape down sides of processor bowl and break up any cubes that are stuck together. Lock lid back into place and process until smooth, about 1 minute. Stop processor.
9. Remove lid and carefully remove processor blade (ask an adult for help). Use rubber spatula to scrape sorbet into quart-size storage container. Place in freezer and freeze until firm, about 6 hours or overnight. Serve.

# CHOCOLATE DRIZZLED BANANA SPLIT

**Prep time: 10 minutes | Cook time: 0 minutes | serves 4**

4 bananas
16 ounces (170 g) vanilla
yogurt, divided
½ cup chocolate chips or
chocolate shavings
1 cup blueberries or your
favorite berry
Chocolate sauce or caramel

sauce, for drizzling
Multicolored sprinkles/jimmies,
for garnish
Assemble the splits and serve.
TOOLS/EQUIPMENT
Cutting board
Knife
4 serving bowls

1. Peel the bananas and halve them lengthwise. In each of 4 bowls, position 2 banana halves side by side, spoon ½ cup of the yogurt over top of each, and sprinkle each with the chocolate chips and berries.
2. Drizzle with chocolate and/or caramel sauce, dust with colorful sprinkles/jimmies, and serve.

# CHOCO ICE CREAM SANDWICH

**Prep time: 10 minutes | Cook time: 30 minutes | makes 6 sandwiches**

Vegetable oil spray
²/₃ cup (3¹/₃ ounces) all-purpose flour
¼ teaspoon salt
⅛ teaspoon baking soda
½ cup packed (3½ ounces) brown sugar
3 tablespoons unsalted butter, melted
1 large egg yolk
1½ teaspoons vanilla extract
¼ cup (1½ ounces) mini semisweet chocolate chips
1 quart ice cream (see this page, or store-bought), softened
COOKING EQUIPMENT
Rimmed baking sheet
Parchment paper
2 bowls (1 large, 1 medium)
Whisk
Rubber spatula
1-tablespoon measuring spoon
Oven mitts
Cooling rack
Ice cream scoop (#16 size works well)
Large plate

1. Adjust oven rack to middle position and heat oven to 325° F (163°C). Line rimmed baking sheet with parchment paper. Spray lightly with vegetable oil spray.

2. In medium bowl, whisk together flour, salt, and baking soda. In large bowl, whisk brown sugar, melted butter, water, egg yolk, and vanilla until smooth, about 30 seconds.

3. Add flour mixture to brown sugar mixture and use rubber spatula to stir until combined and no dry flour is visible. Stir in chocolate chips. (Dough will be very soft.)

4. Use 1-tablespoon measuring spoon to scoop 12 mounds of dough onto greased parchment-lined baking sheet (about 1 level tablespoon of dough per mound).

5. Place baking sheet in oven and bake until cookies are puffed and golden brown, 12 to 14 minutes.

6. Use oven mitts to remove baking sheet from oven (ask an adult for help). Place baking sheet on cooling rack and let cookies cool completely on baking sheet, about 30 minutes. (This is a good time to soften your ice cream in the refrigerator, 15 to 20 minutes.)

7. Fill cookies with ice cream following photos, right.

8. Freeze sandwiches until firm, at least 8 hours. Serve. (Ice cream sandwiches can be individually wrapped in plastic wrap, transferred to a zipper-lock bag, and frozen for up to 2 months.)

# HONEYED PINEAPPLE PALETA

**Prep time: 10 minutes | Cook time: 15 minutes | makes 6 paletas**

1 (14-ounce/396 g) can coconut milk
1 cup (7 ounces/198 g) frozen pineapple chunks, thawed
3 tablespoons honey
1 teaspoon grated lime zest plus 1 tablespoon juice (zested and squeezed from ½ lime) (see this page)
¼ teaspoon salt
COOKING EQUIPMENT
Blender
Dish towel
Rubber spatula
Fine-mesh strainer
Large bowl
4-cup liquid measuring cup
6 ice pop molds, about 3 ounces (85 g) each
6 ice pop sticks

1. Place all ingredients in blender jar. Place lid on top of blender and hold lid firmly in place with folded dish towel. Turn on blender and process until well combined, about 30 seconds.

2. Stop blender and scrape down sides of blender jar with rubber spatula. Replace lid and continue to process until smooth, about 30 seconds.

3. Place fine-mesh strainer over large bowl. Pour coconut-pineapple mixture through strainer into bowl.

4. Use rubber spatula to stir and press mixture to push liquid through strainer into bowl. Discard solids in strainer.

5. Transfer coconut-pineapple mixture to 4-cup liquid measuring cup. Fill ice pop molds following photos, right. Place in freezer and freeze until firm, at least 8 hours or up to 5 days.

6. When ready to serve, hold each mold under warm running water for 30 seconds to thaw slightly.

7. Slide paleta out of mold and serve.

# EXCELLENT CHOCO BUTTER SQUARES

**Prep time: 5 minutes | Cook time: 10 minutes | serves 6**

1 pound white chocolate, chopped or broken into pieces
1 cup peanut butter
1½ cups chocolate chips
½ cup heavy (whipping) cream

TOOLS/EQUIPMENT
9-by-9-inch baking pan
Parchment paper or wax paper
Microwave-safe dish
Spatula
Small saucepan
Whisk

1. Prep the pan. Line a 9-by-9-inch pan with parchment or wax paper, leaving an overhang.
2. Melt the white chocolate. In a microwave-safe dish, melt the white chocolate in the microwave in 30-second increments, stirring between cook times, until the white chocolate is melted and creamy, but being careful not to overcook.
3. Add the peanut butter and stir until blended and smooth. Spread the mixture into the prepared baking pan. Refrigerate for 15 minutes, or until a bit firm.

4. Melt the milk chocolate. In a small saucepan over medium-high heat, combine the chocolate chips and cream and heat until melted and smooth, stirring constantly. Do not allow the mixture to boil. Pour over the peanut butter mixture.
5. Chill and cut. Chill for at least 3 hours or overnight. Later, lift out the candy, cut into small squares, and serve.

# SWEET STRAWBERRY SAUCE

**Prep time: 10 minutes | Cook time: 25 minutes | makes 1 cup**

3¼ cups (1 pound/454 g) strawberries
3 tablespoons sugar
COOKING EQUIPMENT

Cutting board
Chef's knife
Medium saucepan
Potato masher
Rubber spatula

1. Working with 1 strawberry at a time, place strawberries on their sides on cutting board and use knife to carefully cut off tops with leafy green parts. Discard strawberry tops.
2. Transfer hulled strawberries to medium saucepan. Use potato masher to mash until fruit is mostly broken down (see photo, right).
3. Add sugar and use rubber spatula to stir until combined.

4. Bring strawberry mixture to simmer over medium heat. Reduce heat to medium-low and cook, stirring occasionally, until sauce is slightly thickened, 10 to 12 minutes.
5. Turn off heat and slide saucepan to a cool burner. Let sauce cool completely, 20 to 30 minutes. Serve. (Strawberry sauce can be refrigerated in airtight container for up to 2 days.)

# SWEET AND CITRUSY WATERMELON SORBET

**Prep time: 10 minutes | Cook time: 1 minute | serves 6**

6 cups cubed watermelon
¼ cup water
3 tablespoons sugar
¼ cup freshly squeezed lime juice (2 to 3 limes)
TOOLS/EQUIPMENT

Baking sheet
Parchment paper or wax paper
Small pot
Food processor or high-powered blender

1. Freeze the watermelon. Line a baking sheet with parchment paper or wax paper.
2. Spread the watermelon cubes on the baking sheet, and freeze for 30 minutes. Transfer the cubes to a freezer-safe container in the freezer for at least 6 hours or overnight.
3. Make the sorbet. When ready to make the sorbet, make a simple syrup by heating the water and sugar in a small pot over medium heat and stirring. Once the sugar is dissolved, remove from the heat.

4. Place the frozen watermelon and lime juice in a food processor or high-powered blender, drizzle in the warm simple syrup, and blend until the watermelon breaks down into an icy slush. Enjoy immediately or freeze for 30 minutes.
5. Helpful Hint Watermelons vary in both sweetness and water content. If your watermelon is very sweet, you may not even choose to add the sugar mixture.

# HOT CHOCOLATE SAUCE

**Prep time: 10 minutes | Cook time: 15 minutes | makes 2 cups**

1 cup sugar
⅔ cup whole milk
¼ teaspoon salt
⅓ cup unsweetened cocoa powder
¾ cup semisweet chocolate chips
4 tablespoons unsalted butter, cut into 8 pieces and chilled
1 teaspoon vanilla extract
**COOKING EQUIPMENT**
Medium saucepan
Whisk
Fine-mesh strainer

1. In medium saucepan, combine sugar, milk, and salt. Heat over medium-low heat, whisking gently, until sugar has dissolved and liquid starts to bubble around edges of saucepan, 5 to 6 minutes.

2. Reduce heat to low. Hold fine-mesh strainer over saucepan. Pour cocoa into strainer and tap side of strainer to sift cocoa into saucepan (see photo, right).

3. Whisk mixture until smooth. Turn off heat.

4. Add chocolate chips to saucepan and let sit for 2 minutes. Whisk until sauce is smooth and chocolate is fully melted.

5. Add chilled butter and whisk until all butter is melted and sauce thickens slightly, about 1 minute.

6. Add vanilla and whisk until well combined. Serve warm. (Sauce can be refrigerated in airtight container for up to 1 month.

7. Gently reheat sauce in microwave, stirring every 10 seconds, until just warmed and pourable. Make sure not to heat it for too long or your sauce could separate.)

# VANILLA MILK ICE CREAM

**Prep time: 10 minutes | Cook time: 0 minutes | makes 1 quart**

2 cups heavy cream, chilled
1 cup sweetened condensed milk
¼ cup whole milk
¼ cup light corn syrup
2 tablespoons sugar
1 tablespoon vanilla extract
¼ teaspoon salt
**COOKING EQUIPMENT**
Blender
Dish towel
Rubber spatula
8½-by-4½-inch metal loaf pan
Plastic wrap

1. Add cream to blender jar. Place lid on top of blender and hold lid firmly in place with folded dish towel . Turn on blender and process until soft peaks form, 20 to 30 seconds. Stop blender and remove lid.

2. Use rubber spatula to scrape down sides of blender jar. Replace lid and continue to process until stiff peaks form, about 10 seconds. Stop blender and remove lid.

3. Add condensed milk, whole milk, corn syrup, sugar, vanilla, and salt to blender. Use rubber spatula to stir into whipped cream.

4. Replace lid and process until well combined, about 20 seconds. Stop blender and remove lid.

5. Pour cream mixture into 8½-by-4½-inch metal loaf pan. Cover with plastic wrap, gently pressing plastic onto surface of mixture.

6. Place in freezer and freeze until firm, at least 6 hours. Serve.

# PEANUT BUTTER CHOCO MUFFINS

**Prep time: 10 minutes | Cook time: 40 minutes | makes 24 mini cups**

12 ounces (340 g) milk chocolate
½ cup creamy peanut butter
3 tablespoons confectioners' (powdered) sugar
1 tablespoon unsalted butter, cut into 4 pieces and softened
⅛ teaspoon salt
**COOKING EQUIPMENT**
24-cup mini-muffin tin

24 mini paper cupcake liners (1 to 1¼ inches)
Large zipper-lock bag
Rolling pin
2 small microwave-safe bowls
Rubber spatula
Oven mitts
3 quart-size zipper-lock bags
Scissors
Ruler

1. Line 24-cup mini-muffin tin with 24 paper liners.

2. Place chocolate in large zipper-lock plastic bag and seal, removing as much air as possible from bag. Use rolling pin to gently pound chocolate into small pieces.

3. In small microwave-safe bowl, add half of pounded chocolate. Heat in microwave at 50 percent power for 1 minute. Use rubber spatula to stir chocolate. Return to microwave and heat at 50 percent power until melted, about 1 minute longer. Use oven mitts to remove bowl from microwave. Use rubber spatula to stir chocolate until completely melted and smooth.

4. Pour melted chocolate into one quart-size zipper-lock bag. Push chocolate to one corner of bag and twist top. Use scissors to snip ⅛ inch off corner of filled bag.

5. Pipe chocolate in spiral in each muffin-tin cup, working from outside in, to cover bottom of liner (see photo 1, this page). Transfer muffin tin to freezer and freeze for 15 minutes.

6. Meanwhile, add peanut butter to second small microwave-safe bowl and heat in microwave until warm, about 1 minute. Use oven mitts to remove bowl from microwave.

7. Add confectioners' sugar, butter, and salt to warmed peanut butter and use clean rubber spatula to stir until well combined. Fill second quart-size zipper-lock bag with peanut butter mixture. Use scissors to snip ⅛ inch off corner of filled bag.

8. Remove muffin tin from freezer. Pipe peanut butter mixture over chocolate layer in each muffin-tin cup in spiral to cover chocolate layer (see photo 2, right).

9. Add remaining pounded chocolate to bowl used to melt chocolate. Heat in microwave at 50 percent power for 1 minute. Use rubber spatula to stir chocolate.

10. Return to microwave and heat at 50 percent power until melted, about 1 minute longer. Use oven mitts to remove bowl from microwave. Use rubber spatula to stir chocolate until completely melted and smooth.

11. Fill third quart-size zipper-lock bag with melted chocolate. Use scissors to snip ⅛ inch off corner of filled bag.

12. Pipe melted chocolate on top of peanut butter layer in each muffin-tin cup in spiral to cover peanut butter layer (see photo 3, right).

13. Transfer muffin tin back to freezer and chill for 30 minutes. Remove muffin tin from freezer and remove peanut butter cups from pan. Serve. (Peanut butter cups can be refrigerated in airtight storage container for up to 2 weeks).

# CREAM CHEESE STUFFED BERRIES

**Prep time: 25 minutes | Cook time: 0 minutes | serves 6**

1 pound fresh strawberries, rinsed and patted dry
1 (8-ounce/ 227 g) block cream cheese, softened
½ cup powdered sugar
1 teaspoon vanilla extract
**TOOLS/EQUIPMENT**

Paper towel
Cutting board
Paring knife
Stand or hand mixer
Spatula
Piping bag with tip or plastic baggie

1. Prepare the strawberries. Using a paring knife, remove the stems from the strawberries. Cut a small piece off the bottom tip of each berry so the berry will stand on its own. Core the strawberries by cutting a circular opening into the berry, making a small hollow.

2. Mix the filling. With a mixer, mix the cream cheese, powdered sugar, and vanilla until smooth, creamy, and fluffy, about 2 minutes.

3. Stuff the berries and serve.

4. Gently pat the berry openings with a paper towel. Spoon the cream cheese mixture into a piping bag or plastic baggie with a corner snipped off. Stuff the berries with the cream cheese mixture. Serve or refrigerate until ready to serve.

# CITRUS BLUEBERRY PASTRY

Prep time: 15 minutes | Cook time: 1 hour 15 minutes | serves 6+

FOR THE CRUST
Nonstick cooking spray
14 tablespoons cold butter, cut into ½-inch cubes
1½ cups all-purpose flour
½ cup sugar
FOR THE CUSTARD
2½ cups fresh blueberries
3 large eggs
¾ cup granulated sugar
Juice of 2 large lemons
¼ cup all-purpose flour
¼ cup powdered sugar
TOOLS/EQUIPMENT
Knife
8- or 9-inch spring form pan
Rimmed baking sheet
Pastry cutter (optional)
2 medium bowls
Whisk
Toothpick (optional)
Mesh strainer (optional)

1. Preheat the oven. Preheat the oven to 400°F(204°C). Spray an 8- or 9-inch springform pan with cooking spray. Place the pan on a rimmed baking sheet.

2. Make the crust. In a medium bowl, combine the butter, flour, and sugar. Use a pastry cutter or clean fingers to cut in the butter until the mixture forms coarse crumbs.

3. Press the crust mixture into the bottom of the prepared pan. Bake for 16 to 20 minutes, or just until the crust begins to turn lightly golden in color. Remove from the oven and reduce the temperature to 325°F(163°C).

4. Reduce the oven temperature. Reduce the oven temperature to 325°F(163°C).

5. Prepare the filling. Scatter the blueberries over the crust. In a medium bowl, whisk the eggs and granulated sugar until thick and frothy, about 2 minutes.

6. Add the lemon juice and flour, and whisk until blended and smooth. Pour the custard mixture over the crust with the blueberries.

7. Bake the tart. Bake until the custard is set, 35 to 45 minutes (see Helpful Hints below). It is done if it jiggles only slightly when the pan is shaken a bit, and the center is not wet.

8. Rest the tart. Allow the tart to rest for 15 minutes. Run a sharp knife gently around the crust, then slowly release the pan. After you see that the sides have released, close the pan back up and allow to cool for an hour at room temperature. Chill in the refrigerator until ready to serve.

9. Garnish and serve. Just before serving, use a mesh strainer to dust the tart with powdered sugar.

# VANILLA FLAVORED BUTTER COOKIES

Prep time: 15 minutes | Cook time: 10 minutes | serves 6

1¾ cups all-purpose flour, divided
¼ teaspoon salt
1 teaspoon baking soda
2 sticks butter, softened
¾ cup granulated sugar
¾ cup brown sugar
2 large eggs
1 teaspoon vanilla extract
6 tablespoons cocoa powder
1 cup chocolate sprinkles/jimmies
TOOLS/EQUIPMENT
Baking sheet
Parchment paper or silicone baking mat
2 medium bowls and 1 large bowl
Spatula
Cooling rack
Cookie scoop
Small metal spatula

1. Preheat the oven. Preheat the oven to 375°F(191°C), and line a baking sheet with parchment paper or a silicone baking mat.

2. Mix the dry ingredients. In a medium bowl, combine 1¼ cups of flour, salt, and baking soda. Set aside.

3. Mix the wet ingredients. In a large bowl, combine the butter, granulated sugar, and brown sugar, and mix until smooth. Add the eggs and vanilla, and mix until blended. Add the flour and baking soda mixture, and mix until smooth and creamy.

4. Prepare the dough.

5. Divide the dough in half, placing one half into the medium bowl you used for the flour mixture and the other half in another medium bowl.

6. Add the remaining ½ cup of flour to one batch of dough, and the cocoa powder to the other batch. Mix both doughs until smooth and creamy.

7. Scoop the light dough into balls about the size of a walnut and place on a piece of parchment paper. Repeat with the chocolate dough. Shape and bake.

8. Take one of each color ball of dough, press together and flatten so that one side is half-light and the other is half dark. Roll the edges liberally in the chocolate sprinkles. Place on the baking sheet 1 inch apart, and bake for 11 minutes. Don't let the edges brown.

9. Cool and enjoy. Let the cookies cool for a few minutes, and then, using a cookie spatula, transfer them to a cooling rack until completely cool. Store in an airtight container.

# THE BEST FRENCH SOUFFLÉS

**Prep time: 20 minutes | Cook time: 20 minutes | serves 6**

2 tablespoons butter, softened
5 tablespoons granulated sugar, divided
3 large egg yolks, plus 5 large egg whites
1 cup milk
1 tablespoon vanilla extract
¼ cup all-purpose flour
4 tablespoons freshly squeezed lemon juice, plus 2 tablespoons lemon zest, finely grated
1 tablespoon powdered sugar, plus more for dusting

**TOOLS/EQUIPMENT**
Micro plane or zester
6 (8-ounce) ramekins
Baking sheet
3 small bowls
Heavy saucepan
Medium bowl
Whisk
Knife
Mesh strainer

1. Preheat the oven. Preheat the oven to 400°F(204°C).
2. Prepare the ramekins. Using your fingertips, coat 6 (8-ounce) ramekins with the butter. Dust the ramekins with 2 tablespoons of granulated sugar, rolling it around the sides and emptying the excess out into the next ramekin. Place the ramekins on a baking sheet in the refrigerator to chill.
3. Separate the eggs. Separate the eggs, placing the yolks in one small bowl and egg whites in another. Chill the egg whites until ready to use.
4. Heat the milk. In a heavy saucepan, bring the milk to a boil. Remove from the heat.
5. Mix the ingredients. In a medium bowl, whisk together the egg yolks, vanilla, and 1 tablespoon of granulated sugar. Whisk in the flour. Whisk ¼ cup of the hot milk into the egg yolk mixture until blended. Continue mixing the hot milk into the egg yolk mixture, ¼ cup at a time, until all the milk is incorporated.
6. Thicken the mixture. Pour the mixture back into the saucepan, and stir constantly over medium-low heat until thickened, about 2 minutes, moving the pot on and off the heat as you do so the mixture does not get too hot. If clumps begin to form, remove from the heat and whisk vigorously to smooth it out (see Troubleshooting). Remove the custard from the heat.
7. Mix the lemon. In a small bowl, mix together the lemon zest, lemon juice, and powdered sugar, and then add to the custard, whisking until smooth.
8. Beat the egg whites. Beat the egg whites on high speed until they hold soft peaks. Sprinkle the remaining 2 tablespoons of granulated sugar over the egg whites, and beat until stiff and shiny.
9. Fold ¼ of the egg whites into the custard until the whites disappear. Fold in the remaining egg whites until just blended; don't over blend or you'll deflate the egg whites and the batter will turn soupy.
10. Fill the ramekins.
11. Spoon the batter into the ramekins, filling just to the top. Level the tops with a knife. Use your finger to go around the inside perimeter of each ramekin to clean the edges.
12. Bake the soufflés. Reduce the oven temperature to 375°F(191°C), and immediately place the ramekins in the oven on a baking sheet. Bake until puffed and the tops turn golden brown, 12 to 14 minutes. They should still be wobbly; move them slowly and carefully.
13. Garnish and serve. Use a small mesh strainer to sprinkle with powdered sugar and enjoy immediately.

# HONEYED STRAWBERRY BOWL

**Prep time: 15 minutes | Cook time: 15 minutes | serves 4**

2 cups fresh strawberries, hulled and quartered
1½ tablespoons brown sugar
1 cup mascarpone cheese
1 cup plain Greek yogurt
2 tablespoons honey
½ tablespoon freshly squeezed lemon juice

**TOOLS/EQUIPMENT**
Cutting board
Paring knife
Baking sheet
Parchment paper or silicone baking mat
Large bowl
Mixer
4 small glasses

1. Preheat the oven. Preheat the oven to 425°F(218°C). Line a baking sheet with parchment paper or a silicone baking mat.
2. Prepare the strawberries. In a large bowl, toss the berries with the brown sugar. Spread the berries evenly on the prepared baking sheet, and roast for 10 to 15 minutes, just until the berries begin to release their juices.
3. Make the yogurt mixture. Meanwhile, use a mixer to whip the mascarpone cheese for 1 minute on high. Add the yogurt, honey, and lemon juice, and mix until just combined.
4. Assemble the parfaits and serve.
5. Into each of 4 small glasses, spoon a layer of yogurt. Top with the berries. Repeat the layers, ending with berries on top, and serve.

# CLASSIC CHOCOLATE CAKE

Prep time: 15 minutes | Cook time: 45 minutes | serves 6

8 ounces (227 g) dark chocolate (60% cacao)
2 sticks butter
1 teaspoon vanilla extract
1 cup plus 2 tablespoons sugar
6 large eggs (or 5 extra-large eggs)
1 cup unsweetened cocoa powder
TOOLS/EQUIPMENT
8- or 9-inch round spring form pan or cake pan
Parchment paper or wax paper
Cutting board
Knife
Large metal bowl
Small pot
Spatula
Whisk
Toothpick
Nonstick cooking spray

1. Prepare the pan. Preheat the oven to 375°F(191°C). Prepare an 8- or 9-inch spring form pan or round cake pan by spraying the inside of the pan with cooking spray then lining the bottom with parchment or wax paper cut into a circle to fit the bottom of the pan. Spray the paper after you place it in the pan.

2. Break the chocolate. Break the chocolate apart into small ½-inch pieces, and place in a large metal bowl. Cut the butter into ½-inch chunks and add to the same bowl.

3. Melt the chocolate. Fill a small pot halfway with water and bring to a simmer. Carefully place the metal bowl with the chocolate and butter on top of the pot, and allow the mixture to begin melting. First stir with a spatula, and then as it melts, whisk to incorporate it (see Helpful Hint below).

4. Add the remaining ingredients.

5. Once the mixture is melted and smooth, remove from the heat and whisk in the vanilla and sugar. Whisk in the eggs, two at a time, until incorporated. Spoon in the cocoa powder, folding it in with a spatula until just combined.

6. Scrape the batter into the prepared pan, smoothing evenly. Alternatively, hold both sides of the pan and hit it flat against the counter to help the batter even out.

7. Bake and cool. Bake for 35 to 45 minutes, or until the top of the cake crisps up and a toothpick inserted comes out mostly clean.

8. Allow to cool for 15 minutes. If using a spring form pan, release the sides and invert the cake carefully onto a plate. Remove the bottom of the pan and paper lining.

9. Allow to cool. If using a cake pan, run a butter knife around the sides of the pan. Invert the pan onto a plate, carefully pull off the paper lining, and allow the cake to cool completely.

# CREAM TOPPED GRAHAM CRACKERS

Prep time: 20 minutes | Cook time: 5 minutes | serves 4

3 full sheets graham crackers
8 tablespoons hot fudge topping
8 tablespoons marshmallow crème
1 cup heavy (whipping) cream
5 ounces (141 g) semi-sweet chocolate chips
¼ cup sugar
1½ tablespoons cocoa powder
2 cups whole milk, divided
4 cups crushed ice
TOOLS/EQUIPMENT
2 shallow bowls
4 glasses
Mixer
Small saucepan or pot
Blender

1. Prepare the graham crackers. Break one full sheet of graham crackers into 4 even pieces, and set aside.

2. Break the remaining 2 sheets of graham crackers into smaller pieces and set in a shallow bowl.

3. Prepare the glasses. Put the hot fudge topping in a shallow bowl. Dip the rims of 4 glasses into the hot fudge topping, then roll the rims in the graham cracker pieces.

4. Decorate the glasses. Dribble 2 tablespoons of marshmallow creme around the inside of each glass. Then drizzle 2 tablespoons of hot fudge inside each glass. Refrigerate the glasses until you are ready for them.

5. Whip the cream. Using a mixer, whip the heavy cream until stiff peaks form, about 4 minutes. Refrigerate until ready to use.

6. Melt the chocolate. In a small saucepan over medium-low heat, combine the chocolate chips, sugar, cocoa powder, and 1 cup of milk. Stir until the chocolate is melted and smooth but not boiling. Remove from the heat and let cool slightly.

7. Blend the ingredients. In a blender, combine the crushed ice, remaining 1 cup of milk, and cooled chocolate mixture. Blend until smooth, then pour into the prepared glasses.

8. Garnish and serve. Spoon the whipped cream on top, then garnish each with a graham cracker piece. Enjoy immediately.

# ENTICING SANDWICH COOKIES

**Prep time: 10 minutes | Cook time: 55 minutes | Makes 20 to 36 sandwich cookies**

1½ cups all-purpose flour
¼ cup black cocoa powder
¼ cup Dutch-processed cocoa powder
¼ teaspoon baking powder
¼ teaspoon baking soda
½ teaspoon salt
¾ cup sugar
½ cup refined coconut oil, room temperature
2 tablespoons milk
1 large egg
1 teaspoon vanilla extract
**Filling**
4 tablespoons unsalted butter, cut into 4 pieces and softened (see this page)
1 cup confectioners' (powdered) sugar

½ teaspoon vanilla extract
⅛ teaspoon salt
**COOKING EQUIPMENT**
Medium bowl
Whisk
Electric mixer (Stand mixer with paddle attachment or handheld mixer and large bowl)
Rubber spatula
Parchment paper
Ruler
Rolling pin
2 rimmed baking sheets
2-inch round cutter
Oven mitts
2 cooling racks
Quart-size zipper-lock bag
Scissors

1. For the cookies: In medium bowl, whisk together flour, black cocoa, Dutch-processed cocoa, baking powder, baking soda, and ½ teaspoon salt. Set aside.

2. In bowl of stand mixer (or large bowl if using handheld mixer), combine sugar and oil. If using stand mixer, lock bowl into place and attach paddle to stand mixer. Start mixer and beat on medium-high speed until mixture is combined and fluffy, about 2 minutes. Stop mixer.

3. Use rubber spatula to scrape down bowl. Add milk, egg, and 1 teaspoon vanilla. Start mixer and beat on low speed until combined, about 30 seconds. Stop mixer.

4. Add flour mixture. Start mixer and beat on low speed until just combined, about 1 minute. Stop mixer. Use rubber spatula to scrape down bowl. Start mixer and beat on low speed until no dry flour is visible, 30 to 60 seconds. Stop mixer. Remove bowl from stand mixer, if using.

5. Use rubber spatula to transfer half of dough to center of large sheet of parchment paper on counter. Use your hands to pat dough into 5-inch circle.

6. Place second large sheet of parchment on top of dough. Use rolling pin to roll dough into 11-inch circle (about ⅛-inch thick), rolling dough between parchment.

7. Slide dough (still between parchment) onto 1 rimmed baking sheet. Place baking sheet in refrigerator and refrigerate until dough is firm, about 30 minutes.

8. Repeat steps 5 through 7 with second half of dough, 2 more sheets of parchment paper, and second rimmed baking sheet.

9. While dough chills, adjust oven rack to middle position and heat oven to 350° F (177°C).

10. When dough is ready, remove 1 baking sheet from refrigerator. Slide dough, still between parchment, off baking sheet and onto counter. Gently peel off top sheet of parchment from dough and place parchment on now-empty baking sheet. Use 2-inch round cutter to cut out 20 to 24 cookies and transfer to parchment-lined baking sheet.

11. Place baking sheet in oven. Bake until cookies are very firm, 13 to 15 minutes.

12. While first sheet of cookies bakes, repeat step 10 with remaining dough to cut out 20 to 24 more cookies and place on second baking sheet.

13. Use oven mitts to remove first baking sheet of cookies from oven and place on cooling rack. Place second baking sheet in oven and bake until cookies are very firm, 13 to 15 minutes. Use oven mitts to remove second sheet of cookies from oven and place on second cooling rack. Let cookies cool completely on baking sheets, about 30 minutes.

14. If desired, you can reroll scraps of dough to make 20 to 24 more cookies, repeating steps 5 through 11.

15. For the filling: While cookies cool, in clean, dry bowl of stand mixer (or large bowl if using handheld mixer), combine softened butter, confectioners' sugar, ½ teaspoon vanilla, and ⅛ teaspoon salt. If using stand mixer, lock bowl into place and attach paddle to stand mixer. Start mixer and beat on low speed until mixture is just combined, about 1 minute. Stop mixer.

16. Use rubber spatula to scrape down bowl. Start mixer and beat on medium-high speed until filling is light and fluffy, about 1 minute. Stop mixer. Remove bowl from stand mixer, if using.

17. Flip cooled cookies over on 1 baking sheet. Transfer filling to quart-size zipper-lock bag. Push filling to one corner of bag and twist top. Use scissors to snip ½ inch off filled corner of bag. Assemble cookies following photos, above, to make 20 to 24 sandwich cookies (or more if you rerolled the scraps). Serve. (Sandwich cookies can be stored at room temperature in airtight container for up to 1 week.)

# CHAPTER 11: SAUCES AND SPREADS

# HONEYED ROASTED PEANUT BUTTER

**Prep time: 15 minutes | Cook time: 10 minutes | makes 1 cup**

2 cups dry-roasted unsalted
peanuts
2 teaspoons honey
¼ teaspoon salt
**COOKING EQUIPMENT**
Rimmed baking sheet

Oven mitts
Cooling rack
Food processor
Rubber spatula
Jar with tight-fitting lid

1. Adjust oven rack to middle position and heat oven to 375 degrees. Spread peanuts into even layer on rimmed baking sheet. Place baking sheet in oven. Toast peanuts until fragrant and shiny, about 5 minutes.

2. Use oven mitts to remove baking sheet from oven (ask an adult for help). Place baking sheet on cooling rack and let peanuts cool for 10 minutes.

3. Transfer peanuts to food processor, along with honey and salt. Lock lid into place. Turn on processor and process until peanuts break down and begin to clump together, about 2 minutes. Stop processor.

4. Remove lid. Use rubber spatula to scrape down sides of processor bowl. Lock lid back into place and process until smooth, 2 to 3 minutes. Stop processor.

5. Remove lid and carefully remove processor blade (ask an adult for help). Use rubber spatula to scrape peanut butter into jar with tight-fitting lid. (Peanut butter can be stored at room temperature or in refrigerator for up to 2 months.)

# VANILLA HAZELNUT SPREAD

**Prep time: 15 minutes | Cook time: 45 minutes | makes 1½ cups**

2 cups skinned hazelnuts
1 cup confectioners' (powdered)
sugar
⅓ cup Dutch-processed cocoa
powder
2 tablespoons hazelnut, walnut,
or vegetable oil
1 teaspoon vanilla extract

⅛ teaspoon salt
**COOKING EQUIPMENT**
Rimmed baking sheet
Oven mitts
Cooling rack
Food processor
Rubber spatula
Jar with tight-fitting lid

1. Adjust oven rack to middle position and heat oven to 375 degrees. Spread hazelnuts into even layer on rimmed baking sheet. Place baking sheet in oven. Toast hazelnuts until fragrant and light brown, 6 to 8 minutes.

2. Use oven mitts to remove baking sheet from oven (ask an adult for help). Place baking sheet on cooling rack and let hazelnuts cool for 10 minutes.

3. Transfer hazelnuts to food processor. Lock lid into place. Turn on processor and process until hazelnuts form a smooth, loose paste, about 5 minutes, stopping frequently to scrape down sides of processor bowl with rubber spatula. Stop processor and remove lid.

4. Add confectioners' sugar, cocoa, oil, vanilla, and salt to processor. Lock lid back into place. Turn on processor and process until mixture begins to loosen slightly and becomes glossy, about 2 minutes. Stop processor, remove lid, and scrape down sides of processor bowl with rubber spatula as needed.

5. Carefully remove processor blade (ask an adult for help). Use rubber spatula to transfer chocolate hazelnut spread to jar with tight-fitting lid. (Chocolate hazelnut spread can be refrigerated for up to 1 month.)

# MOMS SPECIAL SPICE MIX

**Prep time: 5 minutes | Cook time: 5 minutes | makes ⅓cups**

2 tablespoons sugar
4 teaspoons ground cinnamon
1 teaspoon ground ginger
½ teaspoon ground nutmeg

½ teaspoon ground allspice
**COOKING EQUIPMENT**
Small jar with tight-fitting lid

1. Place all ingredients in jar with tight-fitting lid.
2. Cover jar with lid to seal and shake until combined. (Pumpkin spice mix can be stored at room temperature for up to 1 month.)

# ONE PAN SWEET BERRY SPREAD

**Prep time: 15 minutes | Cook time: 30 minutes | makes about 2 cups**

1½ pounds strawberries
1 cup sugar
3 tablespoons lemon juice, squeezed from 1 lemon
**COOKING EQUIPMENT**
2 small plates
Cutting board
Chef's knife
Large saucepan
Potato masher
Rubber spatula
Spoon
Ladle
Jar with tight-fitting lid

1. Place 2 small plates in freezer to chill. Use knife to hull strawberries (see photo, right). Cut each strawberry into quarters.

2. Transfer strawberries to large saucepan. Use potato masher to mash until fruit is mostly broken down. Add sugar and lemon juice and use rubber spatula to stir until combined.

3. Place saucepan over medium heat and bring to boil. Cook, stirring often with rubber spatula, until mixture is thickened, about 20 minutes. Turn off heat and slide saucepan to cool burner. Let cool for 2 minutes.

4. Remove 1 plate from freezer. Carefully spoon small amount of jam onto chilled plate (ask an adult for help—jam mixture will be VERY hot). Return plate to freezer for 2 minutes.

5. Remove plate from freezer and drag your finger through jam (see photos, this page). If your finger leaves distinct trail that doesn't close up, jam is done! If jam is still runny, return saucepan to medium heat and cook jam for 2 to 3 minutes more, then repeat test with second chilled plate.

6. Let jam cool in saucepan for 15 minutes. Use ladle to transfer jam to jar with tight-fitting lid (ask an adult for help). Let jam cool completely, about 30 minutes. Place lid on jar.

7. Place jam in refrigerator until thickened and firm, 12 to 24 hours. Serve. (Jam can be refrigerated for up to 2 months.)

# CHOCO RASPBERRY SPREAD

**Prep time: 15 minutes | Cook time: 15 minutes | makes about 2 ½ cups**

3¼ cups (1 pound) fresh or frozen raspberries (thawed if frozen)
1½ cups sugar
1½ teaspoons lemon juice, squeezed from ½ lemon
⅓ cup bittersweet or semisweet chocolate chips
**COOKING EQUIPMENT**
2 small plates
Large saucepan
Rubber spatula
Whisk
Spoon
Ladle
Jar with tight-fitting lid

1. Place 2 small plates in freezer to chill. Add raspberries, sugar, and lemon juice to large saucepan and use rubber spatula to stir until combined.

2. Place saucepan over medium heat and cook until juice begins to bubble at edges of saucepan, about 3 minutes. Continue to cook, stirring often with rubber spatula, until raspberries have broken down and released their juice, about 5 minutes.

3. Carefully add chocolate chips. Slowly whisk until completely melted, about 30 seconds (ask an adult for help—mixture will be VERY hot and, if you whisk too fast, it could splatter). Cook, carefully stirring often with rubber spatula, until mixture is thickened, about 5 minutes. Turn off heat and slide saucepan to cool burner. Let cool for 2 minutes.

4. Remove 1 plate from freezer. Carefully spoon small amount of jam onto chilled plate (ask an adult for help—jam mixture will be VERY hot). Return plate to freezer for 2 minutes.

5. Remove plate from freezer. Drag your finger through jam on plate (see photos, right). If your finger leaves distinct trail that doesn't close up, jam is done! If jam is still runny, return saucepan to medium heat and cook jam for 2 to 3 minutes more, then repeat test with second chilled plate.

6. Let jam cool in saucepan for 15 minutes. Use ladle to transfer jam to jar with tight-fitting lid (ask an adult for help). Let jam cool completely, about 30 minutes. Place lid on jar.

7. Place jam in refrigerator until thickened and firm, 12 to 24 hours. Serve. (Jam can be refrigerated for up to 2 months.)

# CINNAMON MCINTOSH APPLE SAUCE

**Prep time: 5 minutes | Cook time: 25 minutes | makes about 3 ½ cups**

2 pounds McIntosh apples
(about 5 medium apples)
⅔ cup water
Pinch salt
Pinch ground cinnamon
(optional)
Sugar (optional)
**COOKING EQUIPMENT**
Cutting board

Chef's knife
Large saucepan with lid
Oven mitts
Rubber spatula
Food mill
Large bowl
Ladle
1-teaspoon measuring spoon
Airtight storage container

1. Cut apples into quarters on cutting board.

2. Place apples in large saucepan. Add water, salt, and cinnamon (if using). Cover and cook over medium heat until apples are soft and broken down, 20 to 25 minutes. During cooking, use oven mitts to remove lid and use rubber spatula to stir a few times.

3. Turn off heat and slide saucepan to cool burner. Use oven mitts to uncover and let apples cool for at least 15 minutes.

4. Set food mill over large bowl (see photos, right). Working in batches, use ladle to transfer apples to food mill basket. Crank apples through food mill into bowl. Discard skins and seeds left behind in food mill.

5. If you like, add a small amount of sugar to applesauce, 1 teaspoon at a time, and taste until applesauce has desired sweetness. Serve warm or at room temperature or transfer to airtight storage container. (Applesauce can be refrigerated for up to 1 week.)

# SWEET AND SPICY TOMATO KETCHUP

**Prep time: 10 minutes | Cook time: 30 minutes | makes about 1 ½ cups**

2¼ pounds (1020 g) grape
tomatoes
1 garlic clove, peeled
½ cup red wine vinegar
½ cup packed dark brown sugar
2 teaspoons salt
½ teaspoon pepper
Pinch ground allspice

**COOKING EQUIPMENT**
12-inch nonstick skillet
Rubber spatula
Blender
Dish towel
Fine-mesh strainer
Medium bowl
Jar with tight-fitting lid

1. Add all ingredients to 12-inch nonstick skillet. Use rubber spatula to stir to combine.

2. Bring tomato mixture to simmer over medium-high heat. Reduce heat to medium and simmer, stirring occasionally and scraping bottom of skillet, about 20 minutes.

3. Reduce heat to low and continue to cook until almost all liquid has evaporated and rubber spatula leaves distinct trail when dragged across bottom of skillet (see photo, right), 5 to 10 minutes. Turn off heat. Let mixture cool for 15 minutes.

4. Ask an adult to carefully transfer tomatoes and liquid to blender jar. Place lid on top of blender and hold lid firmly in place with folded dish towel. Turn on blender and process mixture until smooth, about 1 minute. Stop blender.

5. Set fine-mesh strainer over medium bowl. Pour tomato mixture into fine-mesh strainer (see photos, this page). Use rubber spatula to stir and press on mixture to push liquid through strainer into bowl. Discard solids left in strainer.

6. Let ketchup cool to room temperature, about 30 minutes. Pour ketchup into jar with tight-fitting lid. Place in refrigerator until chilled and thickened, at least 12 hours. (Ketchup can be refrigerated for up to 1 month.)

# HOMEMADE BUTTERMILK SALAD DRESSING

**Prep time: 15 minutes | Cook time: 15 minutes | makes about 1 cup**

⅔ cup mayonnaise
⅓ cup buttermilk
2 tablespoons minced fresh
cilantro (see this page)
2 teaspoons white wine vinegar
½ teaspoon onion powder
½ teaspoon garlic powder

¼ teaspoon dried dill weed
⅛ teaspoon salt
⅛ teaspoon pepper
**COOKING EQUIPMENT**
Medium bowl
Whisk
Jar with tight-fitting lid

1. In medium bowl, combine all ingredients and whisk until smooth.

2. Transfer to jar with tight-fitting lid. Serve. (Ranch dressing can be refrigerated for up to 4 days.)

# HOMEMADE INSTANT BARBECUE SAUCE

**Prep time: 15 minutes | Cook time: 25 minutes | makes 2 cups**

2 tablespoons vegetable oil
1 onion, peeled and chopped
2 garlic cloves, peeled and minced
1 teaspoon chili powder
1½ cups ketchup
¼ cup molasses
3 tablespoons Worcestershire sauce
3 tablespoons cider vinegar
2 tablespoons Dijon mustard
1 teaspoon hot sauce (optional) (store-bought or see this page)
**COOKING EQUIPMENT**
Large saucepan
Rubber spatula
Fine-mesh strainer
Medium bowl
Jar with tight-fitting lid

1.  In large saucepan, heat oil over medium heat for 1 minute (oil should be hot but not smoking). Add onion and cook, stirring occasionally with rubber spatula, until onion is softened, about 5 minutes.

2.  Stir in garlic and chili powder and cook for 1 minute. Add ketchup, molasses, Worcestershire, vinegar, mustard, and hot sauce (if using) and bring to simmer.

3.  Reduce heat to low and cook, stirring occasionally, until flavors blend, about 5 minutes. Turn off heat. Let sauce cool slightly, 15 to 20 minutes.

4.  Set fine-mesh strainer over medium bowl. Strain mixture through fine-mesh strainer, following photos, right (ask an adult for help—saucepan will be heavy). Discard solids left in strainer.

5.  Let sauce cool to room temperature, about 30 minutes. Serve or transfer to jar with tight-fitting lid. (Barbecue sauce can be refrigerated for up to 1 week.)

# SWEET AND SPICY HOT SAUCE

**Prep time: 15 minutes | Cook time: 30 minutes | makes about 1½ cups**

1 pound (454 g) Fresno chiles, stemmed and seeded
1 red bell pepper, stemmed, seeded, and chopped
6 garlic cloves, peeled
½ cup water
6 tablespoons distilled white vinegar
¼ cup sugar
4 teaspoons salt
2 teaspoons fish sauce
**COOKING EQUIPMENT**
Blender
Dish towel
Large saucepan
Whisk
Rubber spatula
Fine-mesh strainer
Medium bowl
Jar with tight-fitting lid

1.  Add Fresno chiles, bell pepper, garlic, water, and vinegar to blender jar. Place lid on top of blender and hold lid firmly in place with folded dish towel (see this page). Turn on blender and process until smooth, 1 to 2 minutes. Stop blender.

2.  Pour mixture into large saucepan. Whisk in sugar, salt, and fish sauce.

3.  Bring mixture to boil over high heat. Reduce heat to medium-low and simmer, stirring occasionally with rubber spatula, until mixture is thickened, 25 to 30 minutes. Turn off heat and slide saucepan to cool burner. Let mixture cool for 15 minutes.

4.  Use rubber spatula to scrape mixture into clean blender jar. Place lid on top of blender and hold lid firmly in place with folded dish towel. Turn on blender and process until smooth, 1 to 2 minutes. Stop blender.

5.  Set fine-mesh strainer over medium bowl. Pour mixture into fine-mesh strainer (see photos, this page). Use rubber spatula to stir and press on mixture to push liquid through strainer into bowl. Discard solids left in strainer.

6.  Pour hot sauce into jar with tight-fitting lid. Place in refrigerator for at least 24 hours to let flavors develop. (Hot sauce can be refrigerated for up to 1 month.)

# ONE PAN FRUITS SAUCE

**Prep time: 15 minutes | Cook time: 5 minutes | makes about 1½ cups**

1 cup apple jelly
⅓ cup pineapple juice
4 teaspoons cornstarch
1 tablespoon low-sodium soy sauce
2 teaspoons distilled white vinegar
1 teaspoon Asian chili-garlic sauce
¼ teaspoon onion powder
¼ teaspoon paprika
**COOKING EQUIPMENT**
Large saucepan
Whisk
Rubber spatula
Jar with tight-fitting lid

1. In large saucepan, whisk all ingredients until well combined.

2. Bring mixture to simmer over medium heat. Cook, whisking occasionally, until mixture turns shiny and thickens slightly, about 3 minutes.

3. Turn off heat and slide saucepan to cool burner. Let sauce cool completely, about 30 minutes.

4. Use rubber spatula to scrape sauce into jar with tight-fitting lid. Place in refrigerator until chilled and thickened, about 1 hour.

# HOMEMADE FRESH BASIL SAUCE

**Prep time: 15 minutes | Cook time: 30 minutes | makes about ¾ cups**

¼ cup pine nuts
2 cups fresh basil leaves
½ cup extra-virgin olive oil
¼ cup grated Parmesan cheese (½ ounce)
1 garlic clove, peeled
½ teaspoon salt
**COOKING EQUIPMENT**
10-inch skillet
Rubber spatula
Food processor
Airtight storage container

1. Add pine nuts to 10-inch skillet and toast, Carefully transfer pine nuts to food processor (ask an adult for help) and let pine nuts cool for 10 minutes.

2. Add basil, oil, Parmesan, garlic, and salt to food processor. Lock lid into place. Turn on processor and process for 30 seconds. Stop processor, remove lid, and use rubber spatula to scrape down sides of processor bowl.

3. Lock lid back into place. Turn on processor and process until mixture is smooth, about 30 seconds. Stop processor, remove lid, and carefully remove processor blade (ask an adult for help). Use rubber spatula to scrape pesto into airtight storage container. Serve. (Pesto can be covered with 1 tablespoon oil and refrigerated for up to 4 days.)

# HOMEMADE ITALIAN WHEY CHEESE

**Prep time: 15 minutes | Cook time: 10 minutes | makes about 2 cups**

8 cups pasteurized (not ultra-pasteurized or UHT) whole milk
1 teaspoon salt
¼ cup distilled white vinegar, plus extra as needed
**COOKING EQUIPMENT**
Cheesecloth
Colander
Large bowl
Large saucepan
Rubber spatula
Instant-read thermometer
Airtight storage container

1. Lay triple layer of cheesecloth inside colander, with extra cheesecloth hanging over edge of colander. Place cheesecloth-lined colander in sink. Place large bowl next to sink.

2. In large saucepan, combine milk and salt. Place saucepan over medium-high heat and cook, stirring often with rubber spatula, until milk registers 185 degrees on instant-read thermometer, 12 to 15 minutes.

3. Turn off heat and slide saucepan to cool burner. Slowly pour in vinegar and use rubber spatula to stir until milk solids clump together, about 15 seconds. Let sit, without stirring, until mixture fully separates into solid curds on top and watery, yellowish whey (liquid) underneath, about 10 minutes (see photo, right).

4. Carefully pour mixture into cheesecloth-lined colander in sink (ask an adult for help—saucepan will be heavy and mixture will be HOT!). Let sit, without stirring, until whey has mostly drained away but cheese is still wet, about 1 minute.

5. Working quickly, strain ricotta and transfer to bowl, following photos, this page. Let ricotta cool completely, about 30 minutes. Transfer ricotta to airtight storage container. Place in refrigerator until chilled, about 1½ hours. (Ricotta can be refrigerated for up to 5 days.) Stir ricotta before serving.

# HOMEMADE CHILLED CHEESE

Prep time: 15 minutes | Cook time: 35 minutes | makes 1 pound

1 tablespoon water
1½ teaspoons unflavored gelatin
3 cups finely shredded Colby cheese (12 ounces/340 g)
1 tablespoon whole milk powder
½ teaspoon salt
⅛ teaspoon cream of tartar
½ cup plus 2 tablespoons (5 ounces) whole milk
COOKING EQUIPMENT
5-by-4-inch disposable aluminum loaf pan
Plastic wrap
Small bowl
Food processor
Liquid measuring cup
Oven mitts
Spoon
Rubber spatula

1.  Line 5-by-4-inch disposable aluminum loaf pan with plastic wrap, allowing excess to hang over sides.
2.  Pour water into small bowl. Sprinkle gelatin over water and let sit until gelatin softens, about 5 minutes.
3.  Add Colby, milk powder, salt, and cream of tartar to food processor and lock lid into place. Hold down pulse button for 1 second, then release. Repeat until ingredients are combined, about three 1-second pulses.
4.  In liquid measuring cup, heat milk in microwave until beginning to bubble around edges, about 2 minutes. Use oven mitts to remove from microwave (ask an adult for help—milk will be VERY hot!). Use spoon to carefully scrape softened gelatin into measuring cup and stir until gelatin is dissolved.
5.  With processor running, slowly pour warm milk mixture through feed tube until cheese mixture is smooth, about 1 minute (see photo, this page). Stop processor, remove lid, and carefully remove processor blade (ask an adult for help).
6.  Working quickly, use rubber spatula to scrape cheese into plastic-lined loaf pan. Pack tightly and cover, following photos, right.
7.  Place loaf pan in refrigerator and chill for at least 3 hours to set. Serve. (American cheese can be refrigerated for up to 1 month.)

# SWEET AND CITRUSY TOMATO SAUCE

Prep time: 15 minutes | Cook time: 0 minutes | makes about 2 cups

1 pound ripe plum tomatoes (4 to 6 tomatoes)
1 teaspoon salt
¼ cup fresh cilantro leaves
½ jalapeño chile, seeded and chopped (see this page)
1 small shallot, peeled and chopped (see this page)
2 teaspoons lime juice, squeezed from 1 lime
¼ teaspoon chili powder
COOKING EQUIPMENT
Cutting board
Paring knife
Colander
Rubber spatula
1-cup dry measuring cup
Food processor
Airtight storage container

1.  Cut each tomato. Place colander in sink. Transfer tomatoes to colander and sprinkle with salt. Use rubber spatula to gently stir to combine. Let tomatoes drain for 30 minutes.
2.  When tomatoes are ready, tip and shake colander to drain any remaining liquid. Use 1-cup dry measuring cup to transfer 1 cup tomatoes to food processor and lock lid into place. Turn on processor and process until tomatoes are broken down, about 15 seconds. Stop processor.
3.  Remove lid and add cilantro, jalapeño, shallot, lime juice, chili powder, and remaining tomatoes to food processor. Lock lid back into place. Hold down pulse button for 1 second, then release. Repeat until mixture is chopped but not totally broken down, about five 1-second pulses.
4.  Remove lid and carefully remove processor blade (ask an adult for help). Use rubber spatula to scrape salsa into airtight storage container. Serve. (Salsa can be refrigerated for up to 2 days.)

# SPICY CHICKPEA DIP

**Prep time: 15 minutes | Cook time: 20 minutes | makes about 1 ½ cups**

2 tablespoons water
2 tablespoons lemon juice, squeezed from 1 lemon
2 tablespoons tahini (stirred well before measuring)
2 tablespoons extra-virgin olive oil
1 (15-ounce/ 425 g) can chickpeas
¼ cup jarred roasted red peppers, patted dry with paper towels
1 garlic clove, peeled
½ teaspoon salt
**COOKING EQUIPMENT**
Liquid measuring cup
Spoon
Colander
Can opener
Food processor
Rubber spatula
Airtight storage container

1. In liquid measuring cup, use spoon to stir together water, lemon juice, tahini, and oil.

2. Set colander in sink. Open can of chickpeas and pour into colander. Rinse chickpeas with cold water and shake colander to drain well.

3. Transfer chickpeas to food processor. Add red peppers, garlic, and salt to processor and lock lid into place. Turn on processor and process for 10 seconds.

4. Stop processor, remove lid, and scrape down sides of bowl with rubber spatula. Lock lid back into place. Turn on processor and process until mixture is coarsely ground, about 5 seconds.

5. With processor running, slowly pour water mixture through feed tube until mixture is smooth, about 1 minute (see photo, this page).

6. Stop processor, remove lid, and carefully remove processor blade (ask an adult for help). Use rubber spatula to scrape hummus into airtight storage container. Serve. (Hummus can be refrigerated for up to 5 days. Before serving, stir in 1 tablespoon warm water to loosen hummus.)

# HOMEMADE SOUR CREAM

**Prep time: 15 minutes | Cook time: 20 minutes | makes about ¾ cups**

2 cups heavy cream
¼ teaspoon salt (optional)
**COOKING EQUIPMENT**
Food processor
Fine-mesh strainer
2 bowls (1 large, 1 medium)
Airtight storage container

1. Pour cream into food processor and lock lid into place. Turn on processor and process until cream whips and turns into lumpy, liquid-y butter mixture, 2 to 4 minutes (see photo 1, this page).

2. Stop processor, remove lid, and carefully remove processor blade (ask an adult for help).

3. Place fine-mesh strainer over large bowl. Pour mixture from processor into strainer and let liquid drain away from butter lumps, about 2 minutes

4. Knead butter, following photos 3 and 4, this page.

5. Transfer butter to medium bowl and discard liquid in large bowl. Sprinkle salt (if using) over butter mixture. Use your hands to knead until combined.

6. Transfer butter to airtight storage container. Place in refrigerator until firm and chilled, about 30 minutes. Serve. (Butter can be refrigerated for up to 2 weeks.)

# EASY HOMEMADE MAYONNAISE

**Prep time: 15 minutes | Cook time: 15 minutes | makes 1 cup**

1 large egg
1 tablespoon lemon juice, squeezed from ½ lemon
1 teaspoon distilled white vinegar
½ teaspoon Dijon mustard
½ teaspoon salt
¼ teaspoon sugar
1 cup vegetable oil
**COOKING EQUIPMENT**
Food processor
Liquid measuring cup
Rubber spatula
Jar with tight-fitting lid

1. Add egg, lemon juice, vinegar, mustard, salt, and sugar to food processor. Lock lid into place. Turn on processor and process until ingredients are combined, about 10 seconds.

2. With processor running, VERY slowly drizzle oil through feed tube until mixture is thick, about 1 minute (see photo, right). Stop processor.

3. Remove lid and use rubber spatula to scrape down sides of processor bowl. Lock lid back into place. Process until smooth and creamy, about 30 seconds. Stop processor.

4. Remove lid and carefully remove processor blade (ask an adult for help). Use rubber spatula to transfer mayonnaise into jar with tight-fitting lid. Serve. (Mayonnaise can be refrigerated for up to 1 week.)

# QUICK PICKLED ONIONS

**Prep time: 15 minutes | Cook time: 35 minutes | makes about 1 cups**

1 small red onion
1 cup white wine vinegar
2 tablespoons lime juice, squeezed from 1 lime
1 tablespoon sugar
1 teaspoon salt
**COOKING EQUIPMENT**
Cutting board
Chef's knife
Medium bowl
Small saucepan
Fine-mesh strainer
Jar with tight-fitting lid

1. Slice onion into thin strips following photos, right. Place sliced onion in medium bowl.

2. In small saucepan, combine vinegar, lime juice, sugar, and salt. Bring to boil over high heat. Turn off heat.

3. Carefully pour vinegar mixture over onion (ask an adult for help—mixture will be VERY hot). Let mixture cool completely, about 30 minutes.

4. When mixture is cool, drain onions in fine-mesh strainer over sink, discarding liquid. Transfer to jar with tight-fitting lid. Serve. (Pickled onions can be refrigerated for up to 4 days.)

# QUICK AND EASY BAGEL SEASONING

**Prep time: 15 minutes | Cook time: 10 minutes | makes ⅓ cups**

2 tablespoons sesame seeds
2 teaspoons caraway seeds (optional)
1 tablespoon poppy seeds
1 tablespoon dried minced onion
1 tablespoon dried minced garlic
2 teaspoons kosher salt
**COOKING EQUIPMENT**
8-inch skillet
Rubber spatula
Small bowl
Small jar with tight-fitting lid

1. Add sesame seeds and caraway seeds (if using) to 8-inch skillet. Toast over medium-low heat, stirring often with rubber spatula, until fragrant and sesame seeds turn golden brown, 3 to 5 minutes.

2. Turn off heat. Transfer seeds to small bowl and let cool to room temperature, about 10 minutes.

3. Add poppy seeds, dried minced onion, dried minced garlic, salt, and toasted seeds to small jar with tight-fitting lid.

4. Cover jar with lid to seal and shake until combined. (Everything bagel seasoning can be stored at room temperature for up to 1 month.)

# CHAPTER 12: YUMMY SIDES

# HOMEMADE SWEET APPLESAUCE

Prep time: 10 minutes | Cook time: 25 minutes | serves 6

8 apples (4 each of 2 varieties, such as Golden Delicious, Pink Lady, Fuji, Gala, or Granny Smith), peeled, cored, and cut into 1-inch pieces
1½ cups water
3 tablespoons brown sugar
2 cinnamon sticks or 1 teaspoon ground cinnamon
TOOLS/EQUIPMENT
Peeler
Cutting board
Knife
Medium pot
Mixing spoon
Potato masher (or fork)

1. Cook the apples. In a medium pot, mix together all the ingredients. Cover and cook over medium heat for 20 to 25 minutes, or until the apples are cooked through. Remove the mixture from the heat and allow to cool down for a few minutes.

2. Mash the apples. With a potato masher or the back of a fork, mash the apples. Once mashed to your liking, allow to cool in the pot. Once cool, spoon the applesauce into a container or jars and refrigerate for up to a week.

# CITRUSY STRAWBERRY JAM

Prep time: 10 minutes | Cook time: 15 minutes | makes 12 ounces

2 pounds fresh strawberries, washed and hulled, diced small
¼ cup freshly squeezed lime juice
1½ cups sugar
1 tablespoon lime zest
Pinch kosher salt
TOOLS/EQUIPMENT
Cutting board
Knife
Microplane or zester
Medium pot
Potato masher or wooden spoon
Heat-safe spoon or spatula
Mason jar or glass bowl with lid

1. Mash the strawberries. In a medium pot, combine all the ingredients. Mash the mixture with a potato masher.

2. Cook the jam. Bring the mixture to a boil, stirring occasionally. Reduce the heat to medium-low and simmer for 15 minutes, stirring often. The mixture will foam up, but as it cooks down, it will calm down and thicken a little.

3. Test for doneness by dipping a spoon or spatula in every so often. When it drips off the spoon in sections, remove from the heat.

4. Cool and store.

5. Allow the mixture to cool completely. Refrigerate in a mason jar or covered glass bowl with a lid for up to 2 weeks.

# SWEET AND SPICY SALSA

Prep time: 10 minutes | Cook time: 0 minutes | serves 6

FOR THE SALSA
1 jalapeño 3 large garlic cloves
1 (28-ounce/794 g) can fire-roasted tomatoes
2 tablespoons freshly squeezed lime juice
2 tablespoons honey
¼ teaspoon ground cumin
Dash kosher salt
Dash freshly ground black pepper
FOR SERVING
Tortilla chips
TOOLS/EQUIPMENT
Food processor or high-powered blender

1. Blend and serve. In a food processor or high-powered blender, combine the jalapeño and garlic.

2. Pulse or blend until minced, add in the remaining salsa ingredients and pulse or blend until smooth. Taste and adjust for sweetness and heat. Serve with tortilla chips.

# CARROT CHEESE SPREAD

Prep time: 10 minutes | Cook time: 0 minutes | serves 4

1 (8-ounce/227 g) block cream cheese at room temperature
3 tablespoons minced carrot
3 tablespoons minced celery
2 tablespoons minced red bell pepper
2 scallions, snipped or sliced
TOOLS/EQUIPMENT
Cutting board
Knife
Small bowl
Spatula
Plastic wrap

1. Mix the ingredients. In a small bowl, combine all the ingredients. Using a spatula, mix until everything is blended and the cream cheese is smooth.

2. Cover and chill.

3. Cover with plastic wrap and refrigerate for at least 30 minutes to allow the flavors to blend, or until ready to serve.

# SPICY GRAPE SAUCE

**Prep time: 10 minutes | Cook time: 0 minutes | serves 4**

2 cups red and green grapes, quartered
2 tablespoons minced red onion
1 tablespoon minced fresh cilantro
2 tablespoons freshly squeezed lime juice
1 tablespoon honey

½ teaspoon red wine vinegar
Pita chips or tortilla chips, for serving
**TOOLS/EQUIPMENT**
Cutting board
Knife
Small bowl
Small jar with lid

1. Make the salsa. In a small bowl, combine the grapes, onion, and cilantro, and toss to mix.
2. Combine the liquid ingredients and serve.
3. In a small jar with a lid, combine the lime juice, honey, and vinegar, and shake until it emulsifies. Pour the liquid over the salsa, and toss to coat. Serve with pita chips or tortilla chips.

# CHEESY ONION DIP

**Prep time: 5 minutes | Cook time: 30 minutes | serves 6**

FOR THE DIP
1 (8-ounce/227 g) block cream cheese at room temperature or softened
1 cup mayonnaise
1 cup shredded Parmesan cheese
1 cup diced Vidalia (sweet) onion
1 teaspoon freshly ground black pepper
FOR SERVING

Flat pretzels, slices of French bread, or stone-ground wheat crackers
**TOOLS/EQUIPMENT**
Cutting board
Knife
Grater (if needed)
Large bowl
Spatula
Small baking dish

1. Preheat the oven. Preheat the oven to 350°F(177°C). Mix the ingredients. In a large bowl, combine all the dip ingredients.
2. Mix with a spatula until smooth, and scrape into a small baking dish. Let the mixture rest for a few minutes so the flavors mingle.
3. Bake and serve. Bake for about 30 minutes, or until the top is brown in spots.
4. Serve with flat pretzels, slices of French bread, or stoned wheat or stone-ground wheat crackers.

# CREAMY AVOCADO DIP

Prep time: 10 minutes | Cook time: 0 minutes | serves 6

FOR THE DIP
2 ripe avocados, peeled and pitted
6 ounces (170 g) plain Greek yogurt
6 ounces (170 g) sour cream
2 tablespoons garlic paste or 2 garlic cloves, minced
2 tablespoons fresh cilantro leaves
1 tablespoon freshly squeezed lime juice
2 dashes ground cumin
Dash kosher salt
Dash freshly ground black pepper
FOR SERVING
Tortilla chips, pita chips, or veggies
TOOLS/EQUIPMENT
Knife
Food processor or high-powered blender
Spatula
Serving bowl
Plastic wrap

1. Blend the dip. In a food processor or high-powered blender, combine all the dip ingredients. Pulse until almost smooth. Adjust the seasoning to your liking, then scrape the dip into a serving bowl.

2. Wrap, chill, and serve. Cover tightly with plastic wrap touching the dip (to prevent browning), and chilor 20 to 30 minutes. Serve with tortilla chips, pita chips, or veggies for dipping.

# ONE POT CUCUMBER PICKLES

Prep time: 10 minutes | Cook time:0 minutes | makes 3 quart jars

4 or 5 large cucumbers, sliced thin
2 large red onions, sliced thin
3 cups white vinegar
1¾ cups sugar
1½ tablespoons kosher salt
1 tablespoon celery flakes
2 teaspoons red pepper flakes (depending how spicy you like it)
3cups ice
TOOLS/EQUIPMENT
Cutting board
Knife
Large bowl
Tongs or 2 forks
3 quart-size mason jars
Small pot
QUART JARS

1. Prepare the veggies. In a large bowl, toss the sliced cucumbers and onions using tongs or 2 forks.

2. Fill each jar with the vegetable mixture, using a spoon to gently push the veggies down to make room for more.

3. Cook the pickle juice. In a small pot, combine the vinegar, sugar, salt, celery flakes, and red pepper flakes, to taste. Bring to a boil. Remove the pot from the heat, and add the ice. Stir until the ice is melted. Fill the jars with the mixture just below the top.

4. Cool and store. Cover and allow the jars to cool to room temperature, then refrigerate until ready to enjoy.

# APPENDIX 1: MEASUREMENT CONVERSION CHART

## VOLUME EQUIVALENTS(DRY)

| US STANDARD | METRIC (APPROXIMATE) |
|---|---|
| 1/8 teaspoon | 0.5 mL |
| 1/4 teaspoon | 1 mL |
| 1/2 teaspoon | 2 mL |
| 3/4 teaspoon | 4 mL |
| 1 teaspoon | 5 mL |
| 1 tablespoon | 15 mL |
| 1/4 cup | 59 mL |
| 1/2 cup | 118 mL |
| 3/4 cup | 177 mL |
| 1 cup | 235 mL |
| 2 cups | 475 mL |
| 3 cups | 700 mL |
| 4 cups | 1 L |

## VOLUME EQUIVALENTS(LIQUID)

| US STANDARD | US STANDARD (OUNCES) | METRIC (APPROXIMATE) |
|---|---|---|
| 2 tablespoons | 1 fl.oz. | 30 mL |
| 1/4 cup | 2 fl.oz. | 60 mL |
| 1/2 cup | 4 fl.oz. | 120 mL |
| 1 cup | 8 fl.oz. | 240 mL |
| 1 1/2 cup | 12 fl.oz. | 355 mL |
| 2 cups or 1 pint | 16 fl.oz. | 475 mL |
| 4 cups or 1 quart | 32 fl.oz. | 1 L |
| 1 gallon | 128 fl.oz. | 4 L |

## TEMPERATURES EQUIVALENTS

| FAHRENHEIT(F) | CELSIUS(C) (APPROXIMATE) |
|---|---|
| 225 °F | 107 °C |
| 250 °F | 120 °C |
| 275 °F | 135 °C |
| 300 °F | 150 °C |
| 325 °F | 160 °C |
| 350 °F | 180 °C |
| 375 °F | 190 °C |
| 400 °F | 205 °C |
| 425 °F | 220 °C |
| 450 °F | 235 °C |
| 475 °F | 245 °C |
| 500 °F | 260 °C |

## WEIGHT EQUIVALENTS

| US STANDARD | METRIC (APPROXIMATE) |
|---|---|
| 1 ounce | 28 g |
| 2 ounces | 57 g |
| 5 ounces | 142 g |
| 10 ounces | 284 g |
| 15 ounces | 425 g |
| 16 ounces (1 pound) | 455 g |
| 1.5 pounds | 680 g |
| 2 pounds | 907 g |

# APPENDIX 2: THE DIRTY DOZEN AND CLEAN FIFTEEN

The Environmental Working Group (EWG) is a nonprofit, nonpartisan organization dedicated o protecting human health and the environment Its mission is to empower people to live ealthier lives in a healthier environment. This organization publishes an annual list of the welve kinds of produce, in sequence, that have the highest amount of pesticide residue-the Jirty Dozen-as well as a list of the fifteen kinds ofproduce that have the least amount of >esticide residue-the Clean Fifteen.

## THE DIRTY DOZEN

* The 2016 Dirty Dozen includes the following produce. These are considered among the year's most important produce to buy organic:

| | |
|---|---|
| Strawberries | Spinach |
| Apples | Tomatoes |
| Nectarines | Bell peppers |
| Peaches | Cherry tomatoes |
| Celery | Cucumbers |
| Grapes | Kale/collard greens |
| Cherries | Hot peppers |

* *The Dirty Dozen list contains two additional itemskale/collard greens and hot peppers-because they tend to contain trace levels of highly hazardous pesticides.*

## THE CLEAN FIFTEEN

* The least critical to buy organically are the Clean Fifteen list. The following are on the 2016 list:

| | |
|---|---|
| Avocados | Papayas |
| Corn | Kiw |
| Pineapples | Eggplant |
| Cabbage | Honeydew |
| Sweet peas | Grapefruit |
| Onions | Cantaloupe |
| Asparagus | Cauliflower |
| Mangos | |

* *Some of the sweet corn sold in the United States are made from genetically engineered (GE) seedstock. Buy organic varieties of these crops to avoid GE produce.*

# APPENDIX 3: INDEX

Printed in Great Britain
by Amazon

15233556R00072